Matilda Betham-Edwards

A Romance of Dijon

Matilda Betham-Edwards
A Romance of Dijon
ISBN/EAN: 9783744692472
Printed in Europe, USA, Canada, Australia, Japan
Cover: Foto ©Thomas Meinert / pixelio.de

More available books at **www.hansebooks.com**

A ROMANCE OF DIJON

A ROMANCE OF DIJON

BY

M. BETHAM-EDWARDS

AUTHOR OF
"THE CURB OF HONOUR" ETC.

NEW YORK: MACMILLAN AND CO.
LONDON: ADAM AND CHARLES BLACK
1894

CONTENTS

CHAP.		PAGE
I.	'THE DAWN IS THERE!'	7
II.	THE SORROW THAT UNSEXES	18
III.	THE FRAGRANCE OF THE VINE	30
IV.	THE BEGINNING OF THE END	42
V.	THE BEAUTIFUL MERCER	53
VI.	THE MUSTER	69
VII.	THE PASSING OF THE DEPUTIES	80
VIII.	A MAIDEN WOOER	91
IX.	CURÉ, SEIGNEUR, AND PROLETAIRE	102
X.	MARQUIS AND MILLINER	118
XI.	THE TEMPTATION	134
XII.	THE CARNIVAL OF THE CAHIERS	144
XIII.	UNDER THE ELMS OF SULLY	155
XIV.	'NOT A BAUBLE FOR MOTHER COUNTRY?'	168
XV.	'THE BASTILLE, THE BASTILLE!'	181
XVI.	'THE BASTILLE, THE BASTILLE!'	191
XVII.	THE COMEDY OF REVOLUTION	202
XVIII.	RED, WHITE, AND BLUE!	213
XIX.	PERNELLE'S VIGIL	223
XX.	THE BEACON FIRES	233
XXI.	SERIO-COMIC	244
XXII.	IDYLLIC	255

CHAP.		PAGE
XXIII.	IN QUIET PLACES	264
XXIV.	SALE UNDER THE DEAD HAND	275
XXV.	'THE DEAD HAND'	286
XXVI.	LOVE AND REVOLUTION	296
XXVII.	'JE N'EN AVAIS NUL DROIT'	305
XXVIII.	PRACTICAL HEROISM	313
XXIX.	THE COST OF REVOLUTION	323
XXX.	LOVER AND LEDGER	332
XXXI.	LOVE	341
XXXII.	THE STRUGGLE	351
XXXIII.	—AND STRUGGLE	359
XXXIV.	'AUX ARMES, AUX ARMES, CITOYENS!'	368
XXXV.	THE TOCSIN	378

A ROMANCE OF DIJON

CHAPTER I

'THE DAWN IS THERE!'

As yet day halted on the threshold of the beautiful wine country; pencilled in grey the twin eminences over against its capital. Like yet different are those nodding hamlets, Fontaine, birthplace of St. Bernard, Talant, historic also, each crowned by church, château, and clustering cottages; at their feet, the proud city of Charles the Bold; beyond, rising with gentle curve, the Golden Hills vineyards famous throughout Christendom. In the luminous eastern belt of starry twilight, Dijon had almost an ethereal look, as if a brisk wind might disperse that picture in cloudland, slate-coloured silhouette against a gradually clearing sky.

Lofty cathedral spire, slightly bent as if in perpetual adoration, as lofty Ducal Tower with its graceful balustrade, many a dome, cupola, and pinnacle, church and palace, gloomy donjon and city gates, showed above the cincture of ramparts, all faintly outlined on a neutral ground. Who that had never beheld a sunrising here could divine the transformation at hand?

Pervading silence matched the shadowy scene. The fair spring world was wrapt in trance-like sleep.

Only in one poor home of the twin hamlet looking west had burned a feeble light through the dark hours, last beam to greet dying eyes. The kitchen of this wretched tenement was windowless, the opening to admit light and air being closed by a rudely constructed shutter. Bed-chamber there was none; and in the farther corner of the kitchen, not too softly pillowed, lay an ancient woman, by her side a pair of assiduous watchers.

So weather-beaten, shrivelled, and burdened with the weight of years was the grandame, that she must have been hideous but for a certain look—dignity were hardly the name, nor resignation, nor the placidity of despair. Still less could her expression pass solely for the vindictiveness occasioned by personal wrong. Mildness, submissiveness she lacked; tone of voice, glance, pose, betokened a nature strong alike for good or evil, vigorous by force both of passion and intellect, consciousness of strength proving a staff on which to lean, a gospel of her own. The pair keeping watch suggested no less individuality. Strikingly contrasted to each other, not in the least resembling their charge, poor circumstance, isolation, pity, rather than kinship, surely linked the three.

Seated on a rough bench by the wall, alertly rising to aid his companion in her ministrations, his gaze following every movement of the dying woman, was a man whose age defied guesswork. With complexion sear and puckered as a walnut peeled many days, with limbs supple and wiry as those of a mountebank, he might have belonged to the ebbing or present generation. Hardship, exposure, a life of hazard, had perhaps aged him before his time; phenomenal powers of endurance, untamable spirit, kept him young. He was short of stature, thin to attenuation, and his small, brilliant eyes wore the cunning, catch-me-if-you-can expression of a preying and preyed-on animal.

The girl so anxiously bending over the poor pallet showed the same undaunted look, and she also evidently enjoyed secret consolations. Her elders could take refuge in the thought that neither suffering nor injustice had power to crush; the light that came and went into this young face betokened solace of a different kind. The two might rejoice in the conviction of indomitable will; their companion owed self-control to other sources. And just as such assurance irradiated her sorrowful features, did her childlike beauty spiritualise and embellish the sordid place.

'The peasant's wife, but the seigneur's bride,' murmured the dying woman, her voice strangely clear and vigorous.

'Again, for the second or third time, those words!' whispered the girl, turning to her fellow-watcher, evidently for an interpretation.

Instead of replying, he rose, and placed a cheap metal crucifix in the large, toil-worn, bony hands of the grandame. Without attempting to grasp it, she repeated the sentence—

'The peasant's wife, but the seigneur's bride.'

'Come, Huguette,' the man said soothingly, 'have done with peasants and seigneurs. 'Twill be all one on the other side of the grave'; and once more he closed her fingers about the symbol. She let it go.

'The priest was here yesterday,' she cried impatiently. 'Would you have him fetched a second time? Godchild, godchild, are you by?'

For answer the girl bent lower, tenderly kissing the wrinkled forehead.

'I cannot see you, darling, but I know your voice, and my thoughts are clear. Do not interrupt me, either of you. I have something to say.'

The pair obeyed: Fortuné—Renard, as the cunning fellow was generally called—not without uneasiness; Félicité—with her also baptism had apparently played a cruel freak—or Finette to her neighbours, lovingly submissive.

Aided by both, the gaunt figure, in coarse, homespun bedgown, now sat up; the final flicker of life burning brightly, lending indescribable pathos, even a touch of grandeur, to the scene.

All the fierce passion and ungovernable temper of the Huguette of old were revived with even deeper intensity. A glow almost superhuman in its radiance lighted up the strongly-marked, time-worn features. She seemed to be gazing on things invisible to her watchers. The face was no longer that of a peasant woman, but a prophetess.

'You did not guess it,' she began, her voice gaining in volume and piercingness as she went on. 'Whilst I lay here still as a babe, I have had visions—not heavenly ones, but earthly'— A grim smile played on her lips, threadlike in their thinness. 'Was it likely I should dream of saints and angels on my dying bed'—

'Huguette, Huguette,' cried Fortuné, crossing himself, 'remember that you are a Christian.'

'The shrift father was here yesterday, he would not forbid me to declare my dreams, I know,' the old woman went on impatiently, even fretfully; 'and as I lay here, drowsing, perhaps you thought, the past came back, the eighty and odd years I can remember, of hunger and nakedness, toil and privation. Childhood, youth, love, these were only words to the peasant. Existence for the like of us meant endurance'—

She broke off, and a terrible expression for a moment replaced the sibylline solemnity that had gone before.

'The peasant's wife, but the seigneur's bride. Do you hear, godchild, do you understand?'

'Good mother, invoke the Blessed Virgin, lift your thoughts heavenward,' ejaculated Fortuné. The girl meantime had turned away her face as if unable to endure that fearful glance.

'He will tell you, I have no time. Remember what I say, Fortuné.' He bowed his head unwillingly, acquiescingly. The gesture seemed to satisfy her. She went on—

'Godchild, if I have been at times a fury, cursing and doing harsh, bitter things, revenging my wrongs, Fortuné will let you know how'—

The last sentence changed the man's look altogether; his little eyes sparkled, he rubbed his hands with a low chuckling laugh.

'Did I make myself, did I make those whose bond-servant and chattel I was, haughty women, bad men, to whom I and mine were mere clods? But listen: as I said just now, I have had visions, I see into the future. Hold me well up, Fortuné. Godchild, a drink—I feel my strength going.'

Rising from her seat, groping her way to an outhouse, the girl fetched a carefully concealed flagon of wine, her companion pouring a copious draught down the sick woman's throat, then slyly putting the neck to his own lips.

'Quick, my girl, back to its place,' he whispered, 'and cross yourself when the good soul talks of visions.'

Huguette revived; she now went on in a clear, penetrating voice—

'I have been a hard woman, neither weeping for spouse nor sons stricken down in their prime. Why should I? The world was an evil place. Better at rest underground. But I was not like a poor dumb beast, unable to look ahead or reason, and I had strange thoughts—I felt sure that even the like of me might be happy.'

Renard pointed upward significantly.

'No, no, my man; I am speaking of the soil we tread on, the air we breathe here. Hear me out. I beheld just now, I behold it still, another kind of world, in which men and women toil, wed, become fathers and mothers, without cursing.'

'Huguette, leave curses alone; pray to your patron saint,' broke in Renard, aghast. Finette pulled his sleeve gently. Tears were streaming down her cheeks. She caught every syllable with breathless eagerness.

'A change, an awful change is at hand. I feel it, I know it. Oh, ye hated ones, the oppressors that have despoiled us and hunted us down, the tyrants to whom poor men's blood was as water, poor women's honour as nought, tremble, find a hiding-place where you can, seek compassion of your victims! A wave of horror and darkness will soon sweep over the land—no such eclipse was ever seen. The very name of France will affright all humanity as one man. But for a time only'—

She raised her hand towards the east, and got out, now in feeble tones and intermittent gasp—

'Night broods over us, but the dawn is there. The neighbours have ever looked askance at poor Huguette; to some I was little better than a witch, because I had strange thoughts and pondered on many things. Even those who sweated with me in the harvest-field, even the women who knew what child-bearing is to the poor, held aloof. All my life I have been alone. Those thoughts I speak of kept me company. Live to be very old, Fortuné; my little Finette, do not quail at thoughts of wifehood, motherhood. Horror and darkness, I say, are upon the land; but following after, days such as the like of us have never seen. Heaven has not forgotten the peasant. It is night with him now, the dawn is there.'

She sank back on her straw pillows, unable any longer to articulate clearly. The listeners put down their heads, and once more caught the words—

'The dawn is there!'

True enough, with the silence of death light

gradually stole over the chamber. For a little while, motionless as the marble-like figure on the bed, knelt the two watchers, a ray of sunshine recalling them to neighbourly duty and Christian ministration.

CHAPTER II

THE SORROW THAT UNSEXES

There is a sorrow, an isolation, that unsexes, annuls conventional standards, draws human beings together, as imminent peril or appalling calamity.

Huguette's neighbours were not wanting in kindly feeling, but her imperiousness, her strangeness, had alienated one after the other. Thus it came about that, except for Renard, who was everybody's friend—even the providence of vagabonds and criminals—and for this young girl, foster-child of former days, she was abandoned at the last.

Lovingly, solemnly, reverentially, the little old wizen-faced man, aided by Finette, performed the last offices. Father and daughter thus brought together in dire extremity could not have showed a completer absence of self-consciousness. Renard, indeed, hardly possessed the kind of personality that at times embarrasses the more fortunate. Hazards, rough usage, keen bodily suffering, and a hunted down life, had rendered him abnormal. He was a human being still, neither devoid of moral qualities nor ethic standards. Just as lifelong incarceration will turn men into automata, so privation and a habit of endurance had dulled his susceptibilities. With the deftness of a woman he now arranged the skeleton-like form on the pallet, Finette mechanically obeying his behests.

During the sad ceremonial not a word was said, but when their task had come to an end, he patted her tear-wet cheek and thrust a rosary into her passive hands.

'Come, come, my maid,' he said cheerily; 'is she not better off above with our Holy Mother and the saints? Leave off crying and tell your beads, whilst I attend to my carpentering yonder.' He pointed to the little woodshed outside, then lingered, casting a final glance at the death-chamber, evidently to his mind seemly and creditable. 'We have done our best for you, my poor Huguette,' he murmured, addressing the dead woman. 'A light burning under the image of the Blessed Virgin, a crucifix between your fingers, your garments whole and white—could a seigneur's lady want more?'

Finette soon heard the tapping of his hammer as he put together the rude semblance of a coffin, cold grey dawn meantime merging into rosy golden day.

Hesitatingly, almost apologetically, she laid down the beads and moved towards the door. The sweet breath of morning refreshed and soothed, but, as she gazed on the gradually gilded, brightened scene, it was with an absent, preoccupied look. The wondrous transformation affected her only as it recalled her godmother's words. Were the neighbours indeed right? Had Huguette really possessed the gift of second sight? Would the day she spoke of ever dawn? Yet to believe otherwise seemed irreligious, paganish, unbecoming an intelligent, conscientious being. There must be another and juster world in store for those unborn, as well as those at rest in the grave! Suffering was surely not the preordained condition of mortal kind? Huguette's lot had been exceptionally hard, Fortuné's also;

her own, young as she was, had meant so far
renunciation only. The things she clung to
and loved dearer than life itself, all these she
must keep secret, give up. Would joy, existence worthy the name, ever remain a sealed
book to many, a privilege of the few?

Fortuné broke in upon her reverie.

'Of what good all the moping in the world?'
he cried impatiently, and, fetching the discarded
chaplet, flung it across her arms. 'Tell your
beads, I say.' With a sharp, almost fierce
glance he added, 'Unless the townsfolk have
made a Huguenot of you?'

'Fortuné!' the girl exclaimed, not deprecat-
ingly, voice and uplifted hands rather expressed
consternated inquiry. He misunderstood both
word and action.

'Well, well,' he replied kindly, 'no offence.
But, like the rest of the people who live yonder'
—here he pointed to the city just half a league
off—'or, indeed, in any town, you don't think
of the Virgin and saints as often as you might.
And there are plenty of heretics to lead astray
the unwary.'

Finette moved a step forward, so that he
could not see her face. For a moment she stood

still, battling with tears; then, mastering herself by an effort, taking refuge in abrupt change of subject, she said—

'I have been pondering on my godmother's words. Do you believe in them? Were the neighbours right when they called her a prophetess?'

'A witch, you mean,' he replied, crossing himself. 'May God forgive her! No, my good girl, let us leave these things alone. Don't meddle with what is beyond us. But if you ask me point blank whether I believe there will always be poor devils like myself, beaten one day, branded the next, now thrown into a dungeon with reptiles and vermin, now tortured within an inch of my life, perpetually ill-used as the saints and martyrs of old— and why? Because, like a wild beast, I seek a morsel of food where I can get it;— well, if you put such a question to me, I am puzzled.'

'You poor Renard!' said the girl pityingly.

'Look you, I don't say that Heaven is unjust, I only say that I don't understand its ways. Were I stripped for burial like the good wife there, the very stones would melt to pity.

Not an inch of this poor body of mine but is scarred and seamed with bruises, blows, manacles, branding irons, and the like'—

'Could you not gain a livelihood in a safer, better way?' asked Finette.

'The poor just light on their feet as four-footed creatures, and do as their fathers and grandfathers did before them. Smuggler, poacher, I was born; smuggler, poacher, I shall die. But a better Christian never wore out shoe-leather.'

'True, true,' murmured the girl absently.

'And up there,' he went on, pointing to the ceiling, ' will St. Peter and the rest despise me for not having a skin like satin and a body whole and smooth as a fine gentleman's? Not they.'

He whistled gaily. Then his mood suddenly changed to almost savage vindictiveness; he shook his fist at some invisible enemy, and, dropping his voice, added—

'There are times, Finette—may the Holy Mother forgive me!—when I feel that I would rather have a bout down below—I name no names—with certain personages, than dwell in Abraham's bosom. Well, who knows? One thing is clear, I must get on with my coffin-making.'

He left her, stepping back to glance inquiringly at the pale, dreaming face. Something Finette had to say, but lacked courage. Him, too, her looks followed, and slowly, timidly, her steps also. ·

'Fortuné,' she whispered, 'I could not put the question to you indoors—near her, you understand. Those strange words of my godmother's'—she shuddered as she got them out—'"The peasant's wife, but the seigneur's bride"—what might they mean?'

Her listener did not refuse to answer, or evade, as must have been the case under happier circumstances. Outcast, vagabond, pariah although he was, Fortuné yet recognised the claims of youth and innocence. Girlhood after the manner of Finette's affected him as the sight of some rare and exquisite flower from far-off, mysterious shores, no more to be rudely handled than rose on the altar of Mary. With women of a wholly different stamp he no more stood on ceremony than the coarsest. By virtue of a certain indescribable trustingness and candour, the confidence of a child combined with the sympathy of a higher, wholly superior order of beings, the eighteen-year-old maiden held him under a spell.

But there is a sorrow that unsexes, a wretchedness of circumstance that breaks down barriers of custom and tradition. Whilst he spoke out, putting into plain words fearful deeds, it was with an entire absence of the familiarity that would have made plain speaking an insult. Finette could listen without shame, he could speak without apology, because she had asked the truth, and he felt that it was her due.

'Remember Huguette's years—and history. Bad as the world is now in some respects, it is better than it was eighty-five years ago; and much as the peasant has to complain of in these parts, they are not so badly off as elsewhere—in the country she came from. Hearken, then —only first let me light a few sticks on the hearth and boil the soup. I don't know how you feel, but I am as empty as a frozen-out wolf.'

Handier than most housewives, he now put together some chips, plied his tinder-box, filled an iron pot with milk and water, sprinkled in a little buckwheat flour, added a bit of bacon fat and a pinch of salt; then, triumphantly hanging the vessel over the blaze, returned to Finette.

'Our soup will be ready in a quarter of an hour,' he said, with brightened face. 'After breakfast you had better run to the curé's. Meantime, about Huguette.'

He took up his hammer, neatly and very economically fitting the odd pieces of board together.

'Eighty-five years, I say, is a long time, and, wicked as the world is now, it was perhaps less ashamed of its wickedness then. In Huguette's country — she came, as you know, from the mountains yonder' (here he pointed over his shoulder), 'from the Velay—the seigneurs were little kings, oppressing the country people, sucking the very life-blood out of them, imprisoning, torturing, hanging as they pleased. And if he escaped with his neck, what with taxes and dues in kind, a poor wretch might toil and moil from morning till night, he died no better off than he was born. But, Finette, we see that sort of thing nowadays. A peasant gets together a few gold pieces and buys a vineyard or a field—all the profit goes to the château, the king, and the church. Now listen,

and hear how much worse things were once.
There was a time when seigneurs had other
rights. His vassals might marry with leave.
They had to get that, of course; and something
more was necessary. A poor man must pay
for the privilege of taking his partner home.
Until he paid what his lord chose to demand,
unless he paid, in spite of priestly blessing and
wedding ring, as Huguette said, the peasant's
wife was the seigneur's bride. You understand?'

Her sorrowful, shocked expression answered
him. He added—

'Such things happened long before Huguette's
time, but she knew they were true. From mouth
to mouth, from generation to generation, the
story had been handed down in her own family,
of a certain Huguette, maybe her grandame's
grandame, thus scorned and trampled upon.
It rankled in her mind, it made her harsh and
bitter, she loved nobody.'

'She was ever good and kind to me,' Finette
replied, with a sorrowful, almost a despairing
look. The world seemed to have grown so
much sadder!

'Humph!' her companion exclaimed contemptuously; 'I have known even a she-wolf suckle a stray. Neither you nor yours had ever harmed her. Ah, Huguette, Huguette! had you only possessed a little learning, been able to read and write, get books, pens, and paper, you would have taught the wisest something, I'll warrant. Now, take off the pot and get out the bread, my child, for my stomach, the poor man's clock, tells me it is breakfast time.'

She obeyed, but so slowly and absently, that he threw down his tools, and, good-naturedly impatient, dished up the meal himself. Seated on the doorstep, each provided with a wooden spoon, they shared the same bowl, after country fashion, Fortuné briskly cutting huge slices from a loaf of hard rye-bread by his side.

'You are not hungry?' he asked, smacking his own lips, amazed at her indifference to the plenteous and, to his mind, appetising fare. 'Come, try again. I won't say that I could not empty the dish, but I would rather see a little colour in those white cheeks of yours.'

To please him, Finette dipped her spoon a second, a third time into the steaming mess, and swallowed one or two morsels of bread.

'I will run to the sacristan's now; you finish my share,' she added, smiling faintly.

'Finette!'

Looking back, she saw him make the sign of the cross, reminder of forgotten duty. Waving her hand with a gesture of apology, not repairing the omission, the light figure disappeared among the vines.

Fortuné, watching her, shook his head and muttered to himself—

'If one could do these little things for another! but no. And all is not as it should be with that girl; I smell mischief.'

CHAPTER III

THE FRAGRANCE OF THE VINE

THE sun was now well above the horizon, and, still dwelling on her godmother's words, Finette paused to gaze. It was not the fairness and growing splendour around that impressed her now—she had witnessed many a sunrising here before—but the dawn and the transformation it worked among familiar things struck her from a new point of view.

Bright and beautiful was the panorama so lately outlined in silvery grey; the broad belt of vineyard below was mantled with gold, warm amber light played upon the city walls, every cupola and spire glittered against the rosy sky.

Far away the proud eminence of Mont Afrique, outpost of the Golden Hills, had caught the glow, and, farther still, light vapoury clouds, rolling off one by one, showed those matchless vineyards, crowning pride of Burgundy, crowning joy of the world.

Not less radiant was the picture immediately under her eyes.

These twin heights on the outskirts of the capital possessed artificial as well as natural likeness. Furthering the work of nature, architect and mason seemed to have kept up this similitude of set purpose. The churches crowning each hill were built on the same plan, with spire surmounting square tower; above sloping green and rich foliage spread brown-roofed, white-walled hamlets. Just now of emerald brilliance showed the vineyards below, of freshest newly-bud green the walnut and acacia leaves, glistening white the little group of buildings on either summit, tiny acropolis of miniature kingdom. The vastness and magnificence of the city beyond—its glorious Ducal Tower, the cathedral spire, just perceptibly curved as if in adoration, the exquisite little spire of St. Philibert, and massive towers of St. Jean and cupolas of St. Michel—but beautified these twin townlings by virtue of contrast. The pair seemed to stand back modestly, pages of honour in attendance upon sceptred monarch.

An hour ago, mused Finette, all was shrouded in darkness, not a feature of the glorious scene she now gazed upon to be distinguished from the rest. The dawn changed everything. Would her godmother's words come true; dawn of other and more miraculous kind change the tearful, care-laden world to one of smilingness and joy? For a brief space the thought held her captive. She lost sight of Huguette's tragedy; she clung to the consolation of a prophetic gift. Oh, if indeed it might be so! if those who suffered more than others could discern things hidden to the rest, read the future as a book!

Appreciation of natural beauty is one of the portions of the richly dowered. Finette could enjoy the soft breath of early summer, the morning beam, but not realise them after the manner of the more fortunate. Aspects that appealed to her must have something to do with personal comfort or alleviation of hardship. Such witchery of hour and season had only half a meaning. She contrasted this sunny day with December, thought shiveringly of icy blasts and task in blinding snow.

The village was but half awake, the presbytery close shuttered. Quitting her high vantage-ground, she strolled downwards. Between the summit and road below, the broken ground made several stages or platforms, appropriated by the village folks for use or pleasure. Here, under the hanging foliage of walnut and acacia, they kept their flocks of geese, gossiped, and danced. The straggling hamlet showed neither abject poverty nor wealth. The poorer houses were mud-built; the better kind, of brick, thatched, brown-tiled, with clustering vine and bit of garden. Below lay a large pond, in which all washed their clothes. Finette struck into a side path, soon losing herself amid the vines.

Hitherto the sight of a vineyard had recalled toil only, weary hours spent under windy heavens or burning sun. For the first time, she felt conscious of other influences, of balm and soothing she could not explain.

Lingering thus, drawing deep breaths of the perfume-laden air, she heard a voice call her name.

Could she believe her senses? Laurent there? Not a soul near, the day hardly an hour old, nothing to hinder brief confidences!

A young man in the dress of a city apprentice,

with a pale, careworn face, joy lighting up his features at sight of her, now sprang forward. On his shoulder he bore a bale of heavy iron goods, which rattled as they touched the ground.

'You were going to see me? But Pernelle, does she know? You are running no risks?' Finette cried, feminine protectiveness, anxiety for his safety, outweighing every other sentiment.

Before replying, before even touching her cheek with his lips, he wiped his brow.

'I have been sent on an errand to yonder village, and by starting a little earlier, got time to see you. No fear of poor bedridden Huguette blabbing.'

'Huguette is dead,' Finette broke in, suddenly ashamed of her joyousness, feeling that she ought to think, speak of nothing else.

'Huguette is dead?' repeated Laurent, he too reproaching himself for his apparent indifference.

Feverishly impatient to relate what had happened, Finette yet held her peace. She could be silent out of respect to Huguette's memory. She could not dwell even on her godmother's strange words just now. Her lover's presence was uppermost.

Uncovering his head, Laurent bent low and murmured a short prayer, the girl whispered Amen, then they felt free to talk of each other.

'Let us go quickly down the hill, otherwise, with these nails to carry, I shall be late,' he said; 'and I have something to say that won't keep.'

With one hand in his, overhead the warm blue sky, around them the waxen green vines, their flowers shedding fragrance, how could she forecast evil news?

'Something that stings my lips in the telling,' he added, looking away from her, his voice, no unmanly one, trembling. Finette loosed her hold, confronting him with a little cry—

'Pernelle has not been unkind?'

He laughed grimly.

'Would that she were unkindness itself — haughty as a queen, merciless as a slave-driver! All that and much more I could bear; but her angelic self-sacrifice, her more than motherly, sisterly devotion! Finette, I must out with the truth, bitter as it is for us both, for all three. Pernelle would fain make me the head of her house. The richest tradeswoman of Dijon would marry a poor apprentice, and not for her own sake, but for his, for sake of her mother's kindred. You understand?'

The bowed head and stifled sob answered him. Finette understood but too well. Laurent was beside her, they were together, lovers still but for the passing moment, for the last time.

'Nothing could be more generous than Pernelle's behaviour,' the young man went on, his warmth making Finette more keenly realise their new position. 'Her delicate-mindedness, her dignity you know, but not as yet the depth of her goodness, her considerateness; none can fitly attest these but myself.'

'You will repay her!' Finette cried, for her part trying to be generous and dignified.

'With deceit, with double-dealing, with ingratitude, yes,' he added, stung by the irony of her words. 'Look you, Finette, that girl has been the providence of my family, maintaining my broken-down, hunted-down parents, cousins of her own, giving my sister a dowry, apprenticing myself to a trade ; and now she is ready to crown the work by according her hand, her fortune, her position.'

Finette listened tremblingly. His passionate words were not all clear, but what mattered the rest ? He belonged to Pernelle.

'The past will be forgotten. Pernelle is grand, is forgiving,' she murmured. He dropped his burden and caught her hands.

'Finette!' he almost hissed out. 'Can good women crush a man more than the vile and the cruel ? Do you take me for a poltroon, a coward ? Should I desert you even for Pernelle—for two Pernelles, did the wide world hold another?'

'I was thinking of your future, your good fortune,' she got out timidly, afraid to clutch at the too blissful truth.

He let go her hands and turned away with the look of a man who finds himself alone.

'Is it the rule of my family, in our blood, to think first of good fortune, next of honour, duty, conscience ? If I did not care for you at all, Finette, should I break my word, think you? But '—His voice became inarticulate, tears made the rest easy ; as children who have quarrelled, the pair now laughed, wept, whisperèd together.

The joy of reconciliation was short-lived. There remained still so much to say, and time pressed. Laurent's errand could not wait, or Finette's either. Hastening on, the glowing day, the fragrance of the vine cheering them as they went, he spoke out boldly.

'There is nothing to do but tell the truth, the whole truth. Pernelle must know all.' With a ring of honest pride in his tone he went on— 'My grandfather died on the king's galleys rather than deny his faith; my father was branded in the market-place, my mother flogged and shut up in prison; their children disinherited, pronounced illegitimate, because their parents would not perjure themselves. Pernelle will forgive everything else but meanness in me. Oh,' he added, 'were it not for this ban, Finette, how fearless and happy we two have been, might be! No more need of subterfuge, my little patrimony restored, wealth for us both.'

'Better times may come,' Finette said, too delighted to weigh her words, wholly unmindful of Huguette's prophecies just then.

'Strange times are coming, that is quite certain. The town has gone mad; no one can think of anything else but the States General.'

The States General?' asked Finette, with childish bewilderment. 'What may that mean?

The young apprentice, scholar compared to his companion, paused for a moment. How could he make her understand? Then he replied, speaking very slowly and deliberately, choosing the simplest, most direct expressions—

'There are countries—there is at least one country over the water, called England, in which the king is not supreme. The English nation is free, and the people have a voice in all that concerns their own welfare. They have an assembly, not like the parliament of Dijon, but composed of men chosen from all parts, who make laws which the highest as well as the poorest must obey. Till a hundred and sixty years ago, France also had her free assemblies, called States General—so we call what in England is named a parliament. Then the kings, even the best of them, grew afraid; they saw their power going, so the mouth of the people was shut, the States General was forbidden. For a hundred and sixty years the only law in France has been the will of one man. Our souls as well as our bodies, our goods and chattels, belong to the king. Do you understand?' Then, hardly awaiting her assent, with a change of voice he added, 'Would that I had been open with Pernelle from the first! But the blame shall rest on my own shoulders, remember that.'

The pressure of his rough hand thanked and praised him. He hastened forward, Finette trying to keep his pace. At the foot of the hill she paused.

'I must turn back now,' she said; 'the curé will be up by this time, and you will get on faster without me. Adieu, Laurent.'

No one was near. Without shifting his burden, he stooped to touch her forehead with his lips, echoing the words. His voice was tender, but very sad. She waited and waited.

'Adieu,' he repeated, and made for the slope opposite. Then she ran after him, whispering in his ear, 'I mind nothing since you love me,' frightened at her own outspokenness, blushing and trembling as she hastened home.

The sun now flooded the vineyards, warming the foliage into gold, bringing out the fragrance of the flowers. Finette was again awakened to the consciousness of a gracious, caressing presence. Nature represented to her something more than the visible, varying world. The indescribable perfume, hardly indeed to be so called, rather a subtle essence, seemed to penetrate her being, soothing, uplifting. Life was rough and knotty, to-morrow would be toilsome as to-day, the future she could hardly beckon; yet she sang softly to herself as she went. The fragrance of the vine came as the breath of a fairer, serener world.

CHAPTER IV

THE BEGINNING OF THE END

As a drop of water under the microscope indicates the composition of lake, river, or ocean, so a corner of feudal France, a single phase of rural life, might be said to suggest the whole.

Huguette, the toil-worn widow, whose very shoes belonged to the seigneur, childlessness placing her under legal ban: Finette, the foundling, no charge of the State, but a seigneurial chattel: Fortuné, criminal of the law's manufacture, hunted-down smuggler, poacher, trespasser; in reality, vindicator of elementary justice—these were not exceptions but types, their like existing north, south, east, and west.

The terrible law of mainmorte still deprived peasant folk without blood relations of testamentary rights. A human waif found upon any estate became the dependent, in other words the property, of the owner. The smuggling of a handful of salt was punishable by stripes, the galleys, death.

Patiently, rather doggedly, as these wrongs were endured, to say nothing of periodic famines, pests engendered of want and privation, and other calamities, there were signs of retribution that those who ran might read. The beginning of ˋthe end was at hand. Huguette's dying words expressed the vague hopes and beliefs of many.

Under ordinary circumstances, the neighbours would hardly have quitted plough and pruning-knife at the rumour of her death. She had never cultivated sociabilities, and to most, indeed, had showed a forbidding front. Only one person was ever in her confidence—the odd little man now fashioning a rude coffin for his benefactress. But solemn news spreads somehow. Long ere Finette's return, the place was literally besieged. Fortuné, keeping his thoughts to himself, chuckled inwardly. He knew well enough what brought these good folks hither.

'A new trade, that!' cried the first comer,

a shrewd, middle-aged man of rather less pinched and poverty-stricken appearance than his fellows. 'Who would have dreamed of seeing Dame Huguette coffined like a lady, eh, Jeanne?'

Close behind was his wife, a sturdy matron, with bare brawny arms, and dusty, unstockinged feet thrust into sabots. She, too, was a specimen of the more prosperous peasant, with bettered circumstances, becoming a trifle materialistic.

'Fortuné can do as he pleases; but don't waste any good timber on me, Pierre, when my turn comes to be laid in the churchyard,' was the reply, the speaker all the while casting her eyes right and left and making signs to her husband.

'I shouldn't wonder if Velours sold this bit of land, would you, Renard?' said the man.

'What Monsieur le Marquis will do, I can't say,' Fortuné replied, hammering away. It affronted him to hear his patron designated by surname only. The most down-trodden at this period were often the most loyal.

The pair, hearing voices approach, interchanged glances. Before other visitors could

arrive, Pierre bent down and whispered in
Fortuné's ear.

'Look you, my man, Jeanne and I have had
luck with our vineyard of late. Get me wind
of this sale, if sale there be, and I won't forget
you. Meantime'—he slipped a few sous into
the other's pocket; then in a quite different tone
addressed the new-comers.

'So you have come to inquire when our
neighbour is to be buried, Father Robert?
Eh, Victorine, how is the young litter? You
here, Etienne! What bird whispered news of
Huguette's death into your ear?'

The last remark was uttered ironically. Indeed, Pierre's greetings had been satire from
first to last. Conscience told him well enough
why these good folks affected neighbourly zeal.

A little crowd had now gathered round the
poor premises, men and women with hoe or
spade in hand, dress and physiognomy betokening degrees of poverty. Only one or two
showed the decent appearance and cheery mien
of Pierre and Jeanne; the rest were evidently
but too well acquainted with grinding care.

As famished herds shut out from lush
pasturage, all stood gazing wistfully, hungrily,

at the tiny estate they coveted, but could not buy.

Innate, inherited thirst for possession, in other words, independence; self-sufficingness, then as to-day dominated the French peasant, was the moving spring of every action. These sunburnt, prematurely aged fathers of families and matrons understood not only the marketable but the moral value of a louis d'or. The gold piece toiled for from dawn till sunset, from January to December, rescued from the clutches of triple taxation, royal, seigneurial, ecclesiastic, was as his very life-blood. His forerunner, Gallic slave of Roman lord, could purchase freedom by risking his life through the enemy's lines, playing the hazardous part of spy. The manumission of his descendant, well-nigh a thousand years later, could only be achieved by lucre, privilege after privilege being haggled over as wares offered for sale.

'Well, and how did the grandame meet her end?' continued Pierre, affecting concern in matters to which he was supremely indifferent. The worthy vintager could not be called irreligious—he performed his duties as a Catholic; but each man for himself, he said.

The spiritual affairs of others need trouble no one. The Revocation had brought about results exactly the reverse of those anticipated by its authors. Instead of effecting religious unity, it had awakened even among the orthodox a desire for toleration. Humanity at last began to blush for crimes committed in the name of piety. From one end of France to the other, folks were weary of legislation as cruel as it was impolitic.

'How did Huguette meet her end?' Fortuné said, looking up. 'Ah, not as you or I shall do, neighbour. She was a strange creature, but a master woman.'

These mystifying remarks failed to arouse interest. Feigning attention, however, each anxious to hoodwink his neighbour, one after another put questions. Had Huguette refused shrift, talked strangely at the last; had she contrived to scrape together a crown or two for Finette, her foster-child? All the time these clamourers for news stole furtive glances at field and vineyard. The longing in every eye was pathetic to behold. It was as the look of sick men at the healthful, of the childless at blooming boys and girls, of the orphan unloved at the loving, joyous family board. The patch of rye, the vine-clad slope, meant, oh, so much! heritage of stalwart son, dowry of only daughter, but they were unobtainable. What with the king's taxes—a civil list of twenty-five millions was not easily wrung from a bankrupt nation— what with dues and tithes to seigneur and curé, the peasant was poorer than in the Middle Ages.

Whilst moodily, almost savagely, gazing on the tantalising treasure, one apparently obvious reflection seemed absent from all. · This little plot of ground, purchased inch by inch with family savings, cultivated so assiduously by Huguette for upwards of half a century, now reverted to the original owner. And why? Because the law would have it so. Huguette, being childless, had no right to will away her own.

As yet the time was not ripe for wholesale indictments of law and system. These wistful gazers were full of wrongs that touched them more nearly. Thought one—If only all these years I had been, like the marquis and the abbé, free from road-tax and poll-tax! Mused a second—If only—ah, if only we poor folks could sow, reap, grind corn, bake bread, sell when we please! Pondered a third—Kings, forsooth! should they not prevent the peasant's crop from serving as game preserve, rabbit course, granary, of the seigneur? The passive remonstrance and stored-up indignation written on every face was more suggestive than any oratory.

Fortuné's voice roused even the calculating Pierre. Whilst putting on a careless look, he had been appraising Huguette's escheated heritage, valuing to a sou, cabbage-garden, tiny cornfield and vineyard. He now glanced up with the rest.

'When folks can read,' began the oracle —Fortuné's reputation for insight equalled that of his cunning—'their wisdom may or not be their own. Huguette, poor soul, was as ignorant as myself; but I have changed my opinion, neighbour. No witch was she; instead, a wise woman on whom had fallen the gift of prophecy.'

'Had she holy shrift?' asked the women in a breath; they felt that, being satisfied on this point, they need not trouble themselves on any other. It seemed so much easier to believe in the devil than in good angels. Huguette's gift was most likely Satanic, but the shrift father would convoy her soul safely to heaven.

'Tush, tush, women! hold your gabble. As if I should put boards together for an unabsolved heathen,' said the little wizen-faced man impatiently. 'Will you for once listen five minutes?'

The speakers fell back meekly. He went on, no longer hammering away, but standing up and confronting his audience.

'We all know well enough that Huguette's wisdom was her own. What she said was this —spoken, mind you, when the warmth of life had almost vanished, when she could no longer see our faces, and only a few minutes more of earth remained to her. "A change is at hand," she said in an awful voice—it rings in my ears still. " Horror and darkness are upon the land, but following after, days such as the like of us have never seen. Heaven has not forgotten the peasant. It is night with him now. The dawn is there!"'

Imitating the dead woman's tone and gesture, he repeated the words, as he did so, pointing eastward. For a moment his listeners remained silent, awestruck rather by Fortuné's solemnity than by anything they had heard.

Emotion, sentiment, show of feeling, were uncongenial to these hard-worked, much-tried men and women. There was a general feeling of relief when Pierre opened his lips. More of a man of the world than his neighbours, able also to read and write, a much-coveted superiority, better off too, which gave him an unquestionable advantage, he broke the spell with a jest.

'Gift of prophecy, indeed! The good woman was thinking of the States General, that is all.'

The universal laugh met with severe rebuke.

'Huguette knew no more of the States General than my sainted mother in her grave. That I can vouch for,' retorted Fortuné. 'But you shall hear the rest another time, when it suits me'; and so saying, he sulkily returned to his task. They might tease and taunt, not another syllable was to be got out of the affronted orator now. In pairs—each husbandman was accompanied by his wife, fellow toiler in field and vineyard—the crowd dispersed. But neither revelation nor jest were forgotten. Folks talked little over their labours; to-day a new direction was given to their thoughts. What if Huguette's words were a prophecy indeed, and the States General—in other words, a free parliament —would stand up for the people, frame more merciful, juster laws? Hope was faint in every breast, oppression had deadened sensibilities, ill-usage brutified even the gentle; for the most part, folks had long resigned themselves to abject circumstance. Yet the summoning of the States General and the drawing up of the cahiers or petitions in every village might well set the dullest thinking. When, indeed, husband or wife broke silence over hoeing or vine-dressing, it was to speak of Huguette and her predictions.

CHAPTER V

THE BEAUTIFUL MERCER

OVER against the exquisitely sculptured façade of Nôtre Dame, crown of Burgundian architecture, under the famous Jacquemart clock, in the Rue Musette, were the open stalls of Pernelle Nesmond, or the Beautiful Mercer—seldom was she called by any other name. From early morning till nightfall, the young mistress of the Coiffe à Merveille—such was her shop sign—might be seen, keeping an eye upon her twin sisters and apprentices, interchanging a word with this customer and that, turning spare moments to account by exquisite millinery. No idle vaunt was the signboard over the door. Here, indeed, alike youthful coquette and portly matron might obtain perfect headgear. Every spring Pernelle performed the five days' journey by stage-coach to Paris, bringing back flowers and feathers, English muslins and straw plaits—above all, the latest fashion.

Too busy for coquetry herself, she always looked handsomer, more elegant, than her fellow-townswomen, so many ungrudgingly owned. She could wear anything; her clear, pale complexion, abundant dark hair, regular features, and commanding presence rendered her queenly always. If quick, decided movements and an occasional ring of sharpness in her voice sent underlings flying, they always felt that they could rely on her justice. The necessity of a scolding would arise every day. Idler minxes did not exist than these fourteen-year-old twins—Berthe, already agog for feminine triumphs and liberty; Barbe, tricksy as a sprite, and apparently as untroubled with conscience, veritable imp of mischief, none but her eldest sister could keep in check. The example of the pair would demoralise apprentices. But for Pernelle's constant eye on the counter, and attention to purchasers, affairs must have gone ill. Her vigilance, business capacities, and popularity made up for any other drawback. The Beautiful Mercer, as Laurent had said, was the richest tradeswoman in Dijon.

Behind this busy, animated Rue Musette, lay markets, narrow little streets with high-pointed roofs, overarching gables, and tiny pinnacles, leading to the Porte Guillaume and the Château. The opulent quarters of the city lay beyond the Ducal Palace, with its graceful tower and magnificent courtyard; between the cathedral-like church of St. Michel—work of a friend of Michael Angelo—and St. Benigne, stood the vast hotels of nobles and rich burghers, the former enclosed in large, high-walled gardens, the latter with sculptured façades fronting the unpaved streets, not disdaining such association with commerce. Alike high-pointed roofs of church, hotel, convent, were of coloured tiles, green, orange, red, geometrically arranged; but severely sombre, the walls of St. Benigne and St. Michel, contrasting with those of Nôtre Dame, glistening white against the burning blue heavens.

A bright and animated scene was that shop front opposite the portico of Nôtre Dame, and under the famous clock. Pernelle's tall figure conspicuous as she moved about behind the open counters, the pretty heads of the two younger girls above the heaped-up stuffs, the apprentices unrolling gay ribbons or showing off flowers outside. All wore coloured dresses, the somewhat crude dyes, and clear, brilliant atmosphere making the whole vivid as a mosaic or illuminated missal. Nor were passers-by less pictorial, men as well as women not being merely clothed, but arrayed, their costumes lending the street a gala look. Hardly more fantastic were those figures high above, the hammer-man, the hammer-woman, and the child, in olden Flemish garb, striking the hours as they had done for hundreds of years.

That clock, stolen from Courtrai by the grandfather of Charles the Bold, was the pride of Dijon. Whenever country folks from the Forez or the Morvan came that way, their first visit was to Nôtre Dame. The wondrously beautiful church—one vast, richly carven portico—possessed secondary interest. Old and young, wise and simple, noble and peasant, had no eyes for anything but the Jacquemart. Children firmly believed that the group meant Time itself, and that if the quaint Flemish family forgot their duty, night would never come.

The clock was a perpetual apple of discord between the Beautiful Mercer and her sisters.

Berthe and Barbe had witnessed the automatic performance overhead from infancy. Day after day, year after year, with their playfellows, they would watch the trio in the clouds, all three large as life, seated as before a table, the bantling raising its hand to strike the quarter, the housewife giving out the half, the husband and father proclaiming the hour.

Berthe and Barbe could hear the quarter and half, patiently seated behind the counter; no sooner was it the Fleming's turn, than away they dashed at full speed. Pernelle might rebuke, customers laugh or frown; with necks craned, and mouths wide open, they stood in the middle of the street till the hour was struck.

But for the last few days the young scapegraces had enjoyed comparative impunity. The city was in a ferment, the townsfolk astir. Pernelle attended to business, certainly, but let trifles go, from morning to night holding brief animated confabulations at the back of the shop. Friends and neighbours were perpetually calling, just to give her the last news, they said.

'It is all those blessed States General,' whispered Berthe to Barbe, as, breathless, dishevelled, on this especial day, they ran home. So preoccupied was Pernelle, so little trade was doing, that they had ventured to the market just behind, filling their pockets with cherries.

'And to-morrow will be as good as a holiday,' Barbe said, clinging fondly to her twin. The pair quarrelled, abused, shook, scratched each other like little furies one moment, were all kisses and caresses the next. 'Don't say anything about it, or Pernelle will keep a stricter eye on us than ever; but,' here she dropped her voice to a whisper, 'she is going to see the deputies pass through, I heard her tell Uncle Parfait.'

'Then I shall put on my best gown. All the apprentices will look at me as they pass; and who knows, perhaps a young seigneur or two,' added Berthe, with a vain little toss of the head.

'I don't care for the apprentices, but I shall hunt for Pernelle's keys and steal a pot of berberry jam,' put in Barbe, 'and'—

A sharp box on the ear put a stop to their confidences. Administering the same punishment to her twin, Pernelle coolly turned out their pockets, and, without a word, motioned them to their posts. The bodily chastisement made faint impression, but Pernelle's silence always augured ill. For the rest of the day the culprits remained glum and submissive. As far as business capacities went, the elder sister had nothing to complain of; both girls were quick, clever, and abundantly gifted with tact. Their brightness and good looks rendered them general favourites. When discipline had done its work, Pernelle would say, she should have incomparable partners. Berthe always found out exactly what purchasers wanted. Barbe as invariably could decide the wavering, those luckless ones who never know what they do want, even in the matter of needles and pins. But the absence of moral balance in both, the insubordination, the shiftiness! Pernelle never wept, weakness she did not know, nevertheless her sisters' training aged and wearied. It was the one burden she could never throw off.

To-day, severity had brought a lull. Mute as the Flemish figures on the clock, Berthe and Barbe now sat behind the counter, rising with affected humility whenever a customer entered.

Accomplished actresses, they could put on a look of meekness that would have deceived any one but Pernelle.

'Ah, good, steady little girls! What a pleasure to see you thus following in your sister's steps,' said a voice from the street, and a tall, angular figure entered unceremoniously. 'Niece Pernelle, have you five minutes?'

'Come inside, uncle,' Pernelle replied, in quick, anxious, interrogative tones. A betrothed could hardly have welcomed her lover with more impetuosity.

Waving his hand to the twins, who began to chuckle and whisper as soon as Pernelle's back was turned, the new-comer followed her into the little room at the back of the shops. In an alcove, handsomely draped, stood the young mistress's bed, best bedroom being parlour, even office, after general fashion. The polished floor was bare of carpet, except for a rug in front of the mantelpiece, around which were arranged half-a-dozen arm-chairs, upholstered with needlework. Carved oak linen and clothes presses, costly inlaid clock and bronze candelabra, spoke of wealth and taste. In a small hanging bookcase, always kept under lock and key, were well-bound, well-conned books—Racine, Corneille, La Fontaine, and a few of different stamp, Montesquieu, Jean Jacques, Voltaire, one or two translations from the ancients, and, in French translation, Locke and Adam Smith. A crucifix hung over the bed, but the almost invariable palladium of a woman's bedchamber was absent. No image of the Virgin, with tapers burning before it, flowers breathing fragrance around, here occupied the foremost place.

Pernelle's visitor was a masterful-looking man, past middle age, of lofty stature, spare to attenuation, slow and dignified in his speech and movements. He had the look of one by no means unhappy, but not given to Gallic light-heartedness.

Impassible, almost automatic, he now watched his niece, as, trembling with impatience, she closed the door and turned the key.

. 'Uncle!' she cried, dropping to her knees beside his chair, kissing the lappets of his coat, the lace ruffles of his sleeve, overcome with a rapture too deep for tears. 'Uncle, I read your face. No need to tell your errand!'

He nodded gravely, yet with a just perceptible ripple in his dark eyes. It was evident that her agitation pleased him.

'You are chosen?' she continued, still on her knees, still caressing, rather adoring, the rigid figure in the arm-chair. 'In your person I do homage to the French people, at last casting off their fetters, determined to be free! Only think of it!' she added, now indeed a tear or two relieving her too full heart. 'My uncles so differently fated—the one a victim of tyranny, the other a representative of the nation. Tell me, we are not deluded, beguiled with vain dreams?'

The armourer again nodded reassuringly. He was not addicted to superfluous speaking. Whenever he opened his lips he had something apt to say.

'Oh,' Pernelle cried, covering her face, trying to realise things by help of the inner eye, 'I thank the Creator of my being that I live to see this day! For good must come of it. The voice of a whole, a mighty people cannot be stifled, as men's voices have been stifled heretofore!'

'Listen, niece,' said the armourer, rising.

Speech to his thinking was a serious matter, he always preferred to be on his feet when holding forth. 'You will see to-morrow such a sight as has never yet been witnessed. Up till the present time, where would you seek Protestants, men and women—ay, for the matter of that, children—guilty of no crime but of worshipping God in their own way? Where would you seek them, I say? Fettered with cut-throats, starved, beaten, tortured—on the king's galleys, in the king's dungeons and torture-chambers, were Protestants to be found; the galley-bench, the vermin-haunted cell, the pillory, have been their abiding place, under Christian kings. But to-morrow'—

He paused, and, still without a smile, only the ripple in his dark, piercing eyes betraying emotion, every word emphatic as a speech in itself, went on—

'I speak sober truth, niece. Twenty-four hours only, and you will see for yourself; true as my name is Parfait Nesmond, true as you are your mother's child, Protestants are chosen deputies of the French people, will raise their voices in the States General!'

For the first time of their lives these two

strong natures witnessed each other's weakness, and were unabashed. Could Pernelle believe her eyes? The stern, cold, inflexible protector of her youth was weeping. Did he indeed see aright? The proud, self-contained girl, in many ways his very counterpart, in all his ideal, leaned against his knee, sobbing with joy.

They gave way for a moment only. Pernelle once more kissed her uncle's sleeve—his new dignity had turned him into a fetish, a demi-god —then, rising, seated herself, and spoke calmly. He watched every movement, not a word or sign betraying approval too deep for praise.

'Is the time ripe for changes so momentous, uncle? May not troubles arise out of such choice?' she asked anxiously.

'Girl,' cried the armourer, at last roused from his stolid and taciturn mood, 'the time is ripe for changes compared with which this is a trifle, less than nothing. You have never witnessed the overflowing of the Loire—I have. For years, for generations, for centuries, the river may have flowed by many a town, doing no harm even at its fullest, held in check by dyke and dam. But there comes a moment when these are powerless, and the earth is visited by a second deluge. I was at Nantes once during an inundation—you have heard me tell the story. On a sudden, before men had time to prepare themselves, the river was in the streets, boats plied to and fro, the citizens were imprisoned in their upper storeys, whilst looking westward it was as if the very ocean would engulf the town. One by one the little wooded islands in the river's mouth vanished from sight, then the riverside villages; then the sloping meadows, till at last only church steeples and tree-tops remained, and still the waters rushed onwards, carrying everything before them.' He looked at his listener inquiringly. Did she divine his meaning?

'So will it be now,' added Nesmond. 'Only'—again his penetrating gaze was fixed upon the girl's face—'instead of a river that has broken down its barriers, a nation has thrown off its chains; instead of villages that will be swept away, flocks and herds, furniture and cooking vessels, it is tyrannies and tyrants.'

She heard silently. Transport had given place to apprehension. Her uncle's words thrilled, but with the sound of a war-cry.

'Uncle, I trust you; you have ever been an upright and temperate man. You will clamour for justice, not vengeance?' she said. The pair were equals. This maiden of twenty-two and the grave sexagenarian, mentor of her unformed years, intellectually speaking, were contemporaries. Her generous appeal was spoken without excuse or hesitation.

'There is time enough to talk of both,' he replied, again with the strange gleam in his eyes that did duty for a smile. 'But the words you used just now—justice, vengeance—are they not often one and the same thing? The sufferings of the people, the bankruptcy of France, must we blame Heaven, think you, or human beings? Suffering hitherto has been the portion of the innocent, the helpless. Shall the guilty, the once powerful, escape when the day of retribution comes?'

Pernelle pondered.

'Our country-people are very meek,' she said; 'even in times of famine the peasant is resigned.'

He uttered an exclamation of impatience.

'But the worm turns at last! Well, I must off and away.'

His hand was on the door when she motioned him back.

'A word about Laurent; I have done as I said—as you advised me to do.'

'Good, good,' was the hurried, almost absent answer.

A question momentous to both a few days before, had become comparatively insignificant; the awfulness of the moment dwarfed personal concerns.

Pernelle's voice roused him. In a tone of apology she added—

'Of myself I do not think, I have no scruple. But the children's prospects—will my twins suffer?'

Parfait laughed away the misgiving.

'The law proclaimed Laurent his father's son, in other words, declared the heretic a citizen, a year ago. The States General will do the rest. Who knows? Ere those minxes yonder are grown up, my nephew, your husband, may have got back his own, the lands confiscated by the Revocation? As to other matters, you and I, niece, are pretty much of one mind, I think. We look first to what a man does, next to what he believes—

examine his life before we pick his creed to pieces.'

He kissed her on the forehead, and, nodding to the giglets behind the counter, hastened off.

'Those blessed States General!' whispered Barbe to Berthe. 'Look at sister Pernelle; she is no more minding us than the figures on the clock. So one more game of dominoes, darling!'

CHAPTER VI

THE MUSTER

NEXT morning dawned appropriately. The peerless day befitted the splendid occasion. Only light clouds just tinted with pink and gold floated about the dazzling heavens, only soft breaths were wafted from flowering vineyard and piny hills. Never had the proud city of Dijon shown to greater advantage; its close-set towers and pinnacles shining in the sun, the curved spire of St. Bénigne towering above all, and—was it mere fancy?—to-day more perceptibly bent, as if to join in the general thanksgiving.

The trio striking the hours in cloudland, as they had struck them since the days of Charles the Bold, looked down on a spectacle not to be matched in their experiences. Certes, yonder Fleming and his spouse must have seen many a wondrous sight during the long spell of centuries, none that could compare with this; yet they held their seats, automatically giving out the hours, only—so thought some—with more than usual alacrity and sonorousness. Keeping the hammer-man and hammer-woman company—better still, stationed on the Ducal Tower close by—a spectator would have gained an image of the ocean. Few indeed of the crowds present had ever beheld the Mediterranean, much less the Atlantic. To-day they were in presence of a living sea, an ever-swelling, ever-growing tide of human heads. From all directions and by all kinds of conveyances folks came, many had made long journeys on foot, the poorest wearing holiday garb.

As each stream of sightseers issued from the city gates, it was curious to notice how they differed, north, south, east, and west sending its special contingent, each having strongly-marked characteristic. The western gate disgorged a prosperous crowd, wealthy vintagers and wine-merchants from the graceful, half Flemish little town of Beaune, barge-owners, shipwrights, and timber merchants from Seurre, heroic St. Jean de Losne, and Auxonne, so daintily placed

on the Saône, all in semi-Quakerish garb;
they wore three-cornered felt hats, black cloth
redingotes, or frock-coats, of English pattern,
long-lappeted waistcoats of bright colour and
rich stuff, dark breeches and stockings, one
pair worn over another to improve the shape
of the leg.

Not of wholly unprosperous appearance were
the peasants from the same region, with clothes
of coarse homespun, but neither ragged nor
unseemly; some wore sabots, others shoes, which
for economy's sake they had carried until
entering the town. Their headgear consisted
of the red woollen cap usually worn by country-
men at this time, so soon to be made symbolic
of equality before the law, also, alas! of violence
inseparable from revolution. These small
vintagers and farmers had a certain polished,
cosmopolitan air, as of men accustomed to cities.
Of very different appearance were the shep-
herds of the Morvan, their looks astounding the
town's folk. For the first time these uncouth
strangers evidently beheld glittering booths,
nobles in velvet and gold lace, ladies in sedan
chairs, hotels and palaces; and as certainly for
the first time most Dijonnais elbowed such

neighbours. Vercingetorix and his followers seemed alive again, spirited from the grave to acclaim the dawn of freedom! The highlanders of Château Chinon were attired much after the fashion of their haughty forerunners, those men who 'feared not death,' and for seven years kept Cæsar at bay. Over their broad shoulders they wore the short Gallic *sagum*, or cloak of undressed goatskin or rough plaid; armlets and anklets, painted shield and lance, would have completed the illusion.

Contrasted alike with burly citizens and wild mountaineers, were small processions from Flavigny and Citeaux, attenuated Dominicans in their white robes, walking with heads bowed down, reading as they went; rubicund, plump Franciscans in brown robe and white girdle, airily chatting, glad to feel themselves in a crowd.

Conspicuous groups also were the rich corporations, butchers of Semur, ironmasters of Creuzot, corn merchants of the Plat de Langres, or great eastern plain. Each little company kept together, the representatives exciting general admiration on account of their well-known opulence. Although dressed after the manner of other folks, all were recognised, certain callings, as we know, stamping appearance and physiognomy.

Mingling with the crowd, sightseers in their best, townsfolk in gala dress, the city itself decked out with garlands and gay draperies, were furtive, slouching figures that seemed to shun the day, as if conscious of putting it to shame.

Wan, livid, almost spectral in their hollow-eyed meagreness, their tattered clothes hardly answering the purposes of decency, these men, women, and children but vaguely suggested humankind. They looked rather like some intermediate species, a race appertaining neither to the higher nor lower, appealing to feelings alike of horror and pity.

As a dark thread running through gorgeous embroidery, the poverty-stricken, the vagabond and the outlaw, shared the festival.

'Quick, Barbe! a loaf of bread and broken meat for the poor. Berthe, fetch my reticule; and mind, give each of you a sou of your own to the next beggar,' cried Pernelle, as, her toilette finished, she entered the shop.

Little business was doing, but the open

mercers' and drapers' stalls with their display of goods added gaiety to the scene, and, stationed in front, their owners could see and hear all that was going on. For the most part, apprentices and serving people were accorded a holiday.

Pernelle and her sisters made a captivating group. The Beautiful Mercer, never shrinking from an initiative, wore a plain white muslin gown, Parisian fashion, lately introduced by Creole ladies, and in high favour at court.

Berthe and Barbe, already coquettes to the finger-tip, looked as if they had just walked out of Watteau's canvas. They wore fine Indian cambrics spotted with pale yellow, pointed waists, short sleeves, and balloon-like upper skirts open at the front; crowning piled up hair, quaint coif, half bonnet, half cap, tied under the chin, high-heeled shoes, primrose-coloured stockings dotted with black, and long mittens made up the costume.

Whilst Pernelle remained unmindful of her new attire, the twins showed their appreciation every moment. Words, looks, gestures became artificial, no less adjuncts of finery than pins and tags.

To behold Berthe waiting on a customer was as good as a play. Not a feature, not a muscle, but now acted a part. As to Barbe, for once the incorrigible hoyden and trickster was subdued, positively awed into feminine self-consciousness, by virtue of fashionable dress. She moved about demurely, even timidly, as if fearing lest at every step this new, exquisite self would come to pieces.

'You poor old man, here is bread for you, ay, and money too,' Pernelle said, as an abject figure hobbled up. 'Heaven forbid that any should go hungry on such a day!'

From her beautiful, expressive hand fell one coin after another into the dilapidated hat held out. Then, with a startled look, she whispered—

'You, Fortuné, and thus disguised?'

What with crutches, fictitious scars and feigned infirmities, the bundle of rags before her was indeed unrecognisable. The muscular, agile little man of fifty and odd years looked at least fourscore. Just then the twins were otherwise engaged. Berthe had caught sight of an unusually engaging neighbour, the handsome hairdresser's apprentice over the way.

Barbe was concernedly readjusting her head-dress before a pocket mirror.

The pretended beggar, laughing in his sleeve, chuckling at sight of soldiers keeping guard close by, bent low and whispered—

'Yonder gentry would pounce on me as hunting dog on a hare, did they know. But, my fine gentlemen, Fortuné has had enough of the executioner's preliminary attentions; he won't die at his hands if he can help it! A word, then, and I am off. Huguette is dead. You will have back your little serving-maid to-morrow.'

'One moment!' Pernelle cried, slipping a louis-d'or into his palm. 'Huguette was friendless and very poor; she mothered one lonelier, poorer than herself; let her be decently buried.'

The smuggler's keen eyes gleamed from under his slouched hat, and he uttered an ejaculation, but not wholly of gratitude or pleasure. Cunning and self-approval betrayed themselves in look and gesture as he pocketed the gold piece, then limped away.

Pernelle watched him pityingly. 'Oh,' she thought, 'that there should be human beings so hunted down, so mercilessly treated, in this great, this so-called Christian France! And for what crimes, forsooth! these daily tortures we witness--the branding-iron, the whipping-post, the rack? In Fortuné's, case miserable little thefts only—a handful of the king's salt, a head of the seigneur's game; in the case of others, a contraband prayer, a smuggled psalm-singing!'

She watched the tatterdemalion disappear, soon to be lost amid the gay, vivacious crowd; her own thoughts as quickly merged in others of cheerfuller kind.

Fortuné was far from pitying himself at that particular moment; on the contrary, perhaps no' one more thoroughly enjoyed the pervading bustle and excitement than this escaped gallows-bird, this defier of the king's law and its ministers. Folks showed themselves generous to any one of unusually wretched appearance; a prosperous citizen's dame here gave the apparently blind, halting figure a coin; comfortable-looking merchants treated him to a glass of Bordeaux. With pocket well filled and heart well warmed, the smuggler, poacher, and blockade-runner in general, as he might be called, leisurely made his rounds.

What especially exhilarated him was the handsome gabled façade of the Parliament prison, to-day a mass of grey walls and nothing more, on former occasions scene of direst bodily anguish and privation. With true Gallic bravado he now apostrophised the horrible place, giving it personality, shaking his fist as at living antagonist.

'Good day, Madam Prison. I hope I see you well,' he murmured. 'I am invited inside? Thank you kindly, the invitation will keep.'

He made grimace after grimace. 'Ah, hussy! I know you, better than you know Renard, that I can vouchsafe. Get your nice little contrivances for opening men's mouths ready, put the very imps of darkness to shame with your inventions. My tongue is my own. Fortuné will neither betray himself nor his comrades so long as he remains in his senses, master of his will.'

He rubbed this limb and that, recalling chains, lashes, and inflictions more terrible still, a grim self-congratulatory smile on his lips the while. 'Yes,' he mused; 'to be free of aches, pains, lacerations, and bruises is a heaven upon earth; to have worsted one's tormentors, as good as a rest on Abraham's bosom. Adieu, Madam Prison. I may make your further acquaintance, to my cost. Your ladyship will get no confidences from her humble servant.'

Bowing low, the cynical jester turned away; entering St. Michel's, he then solemnly performed his devotions.

CHAPTER VII

THE PASSING OF THE DEPUTIES

STILL the crowds thickened. All Burgundy, all France, seemed bent on greeting the deputies as they passed, on wishing the elected of the people God-speed. By midday the streets wore an unprecedented appearance. Never within living memory had such a concourse been seen, never had general expectation been raised to such a pitch. In feverish impatience the vast multitude waited, all eyes strained towards one point, all ears hearkening for one sound. The post-horses from the south, the mail-coaches from Lyons, St. Etienne, Grenoble, the great cities of the Rhône valley, why did they tarry? Dijon must be passed on the way to Paris. So folks comforted themselves; earlier or later, the deputies were sure to drive through the town. Underlying this unanimity, this naïve inquisitiveness, were of course mixed feelings and passions. The throngs now jostling each other good-naturedly as at a raree-show, did not more strikingly differ in dress, looks, manner, and speech, than in opinions. To-day class prejudices and animosities came very close together. The stickler by tradition, the upholder of autocratic and priestly rule, of absolutism in politics and theology, elbowed reformer and rationalist, advocates of legal equality and religious tolerance. Here stood a disciple of Voltaire, a clamourer for Habeas Corpus, free press, and freedom of discussion; there an adherent of Bossuet, staunch believer in the divine right of kings, the supremacy of the Church, the subjection of the masses.

In imposing, to some, indeed, it seemed awful, array, were marshalled the aristocracy of the gown, the violet-robed, ermined administrators of the law and members of the Burgundian parliament. Judges and legislators, hitherto umpires of the people's destiny, had come to hail the new era, by a strange irony of fortune acclaiming their own downfall, welcoming overthrow.

To-day, as it might seem, none thought

of results; every mind was concentrated on the event of the hour. Social feuds, class prejudices, opposed dogma, were merged in an immense, a magnanimous curiosity. The great sight made all brethren and sisters. The great sight—of nothing, of everything? What had an entire province mustered to see? Only a few fellow-citizens, two-thirds of these plain, homely bourgeois, transformed by circumstances into heroes, rendered august by a name!

At last, none knew who gave it, the signal came. For a brief interval the tens of thousands were hushed as one man; from end to end, the living stream coiled round the heart of the town, was mute and stock-still; then it swayed with slow, serpentine movements, and a murmur arose, drowning the noise of wheels and postillion's whips. Wave upon wave of sound increased the volume; soon the low, monotonous murmur grew to a roar of mingled voices, as huge breakers that dash upon the shore; each many-throated, far-echoed shout became more deafening than the last.

'Oh, Pernelle!' cried Berthe, in tears. To her discomfiture, the hairdresser's apprentice had just moved away, the block of spectators around seemed on the point of breaking up. 'I said from the first we should see nothing here!'

'Peace, child!' was the absent reply; but Barbe, taking advantage of her elder sister's preoccupation, motioned the other to follow her. Away flew both, pushing, squeezing, elbowing a passage through the crowd.

Pernelle had hardly noticed the dereliction till reminded of it by her somewhat crusty apprentice. She only answered with an impatient little shrug of the shoulders—eyes, fancy, conjecture busy with weightier things. Another incident was as summarily dismissed. Laurent now came up, dressed in holiday attire, and stood before her, making respectful, even humble obeisance. She returned his greeting automatically, then held up one hand enjoining silence. The young man moved aside, unsubdued by her beauty, only partially alive to the momentous occasion, his mind full of dread and misgiving.

No poltroon was this ironmaster's apprentice; unmalleable as metal resisting his hammer, the will inherited of Huguenot ancestors.

Pernelle, rich, held in honour, generous; he was penniless, an outlaw, her protégé. He trembled before the self-inflicted stigma of ingratitude and its consequences to another. Deprived of his cousin's patronage, thrown upon the world without money, without friends, under a social ban, what would become of him? And Finette? To her also this noble girl had been a providence, a good genius.

Pernelle's cry roused him from self, and what seemed suddenly transformed to petty cares. There was a trumpet-like ring in her voice as she hailed the approach of wheels.

'They come, they come!' she exclaimed. 'The representatives of the people, the saviours of our country!'

Then, suppressing a sob, overcoming emotion by an effort, she took up a basket of flowers and awaited the arrival, rigid as caryatid with corbel. Berthe and Barbe were to have offered the lilies and roses, but the twins were out of sight. To them this great day meant only a holiday, gala dress, and brief escape from Pernelle's stern rule.

Amid tremendous huzzas, waving of hats and handkerchiefs, and clapping of hands, the first post-chaise now drew up; a huge berline drawn by four sturdy horses, every place occupied. The lumbering, dilapidated old vehicle might have served as an image of the *ancien régime* its inmates were about to break up. How these crazy sides and creaking wheels held together, thus freighted, was little short of miracle. Closely packed inside and out, by the aid of extra relays, the berline had, however, performed the long journey from Languedoc with even greater speed than usual.

With a single exception, the travellers were of sufficiently familiar appearance. Just such a contingent might pass through the town any day. No stage-coach but carried abbés, merchants, notaries, wine-growers; and cheers rose from the crowd as one calling was recognised after another. Men carry their business about with them; and although dressed alike, the sheep-farmer ran no risk of being taken for a university professor, nor the man of law, although in ordinary dress, for a tallow-chandler. The sober bourgeois costume, borrowed from England, now uniformly worn by the middle classes and even nobility of France, could not do away with certain tell-tale characteristics.

One fare for a moment puzzled bystanders.

Who could be that figure wearing semi-clerical garb, of semi-clerical aspect, yet untonsured, having neither crucifix at his girdle nor breviary in his hand? Folks stared, tittered, nudged each other, as light broke upon their minds.

Was the man, forsooth, a Huguenot, a heretic, self-styled minister of schismatic church? asked some. To others occurred a different thought. Were the States General already undoing the work of that terrible Revocation, the doom of millions, the ruin of France? Had men's convictions for once and for all ceased to be crimes, only yesterday punishable by the rack and the wheel?

Meantime, the subject of so much guesswork kept his seat, looking about him silently and sadly. A curé, fellow-traveller and fellow-deputy, was now helped, rather lifted out, and borne in triumph to the post-house, women kissing his hands and garments, mothers holding up babes to be blessed. Another passenger, portly corn-dealer, with much of the rustic about him, was as vociferously welcomed by customers and friends. A third, village notary, and utter stranger in the place, found himself no less of a hero, all the notaries of Bourgogne seemed there to acclaim a colleague. He too was taken off his feet.

As one by one the travellers alighted for bite and sup, each was royally received, only the sad, dignified figure in semi-ecclesiastical dress being left unfêted and alone.

Quite suddenly the situation changed: the moment belonged to him, none had eyes, ears, voice for the cynosures of a few seconds before. A cry of supreme joyousness rent the air, it was as if the pent-up transport of countless hearts found expression, the passion of thousands thrilled a single voice; then two figures, one tall and manly, the other fair, white-robed as a bride, were bending low before the pariah, asking a blessing of the outlaw.

Laurent had forgotten everything — his patroness's probable displeasure, his master's indignation, worldly ruin. At sight of this unknown country pastor, now chosen as a representative of the people, he acclaimed the dawn of religious liberty, he did homage to that great principle for which his fathers had confronted every earthly ill, forfeited their substance, poured out their blood.

Kneeling thus, unable to check sobs of thanksgiving, he felt a woman's hand steal into his own, hold it fast with encouraging, protective grasp. For a moment Pernelle had remained inert as sculptured nymph, her flowers held passively, her lips parted in radiant smile. All at once the marble breathed, moved, but it was no smiling Flora kindled into passionate life, rather the goddess of Hope seemed there, beautiful impersonation of trust and looking forward.

Her lilies of the valley and early roses fell to the ground as a thank-offering, and—could folks believe their eyes? To the astoundment of the citizens and the perplexity of lookers-on, the foremost Dijonnaise, the fairest maiden present, was doing reverence to a make-believe priest, tacitly acknowledging a heterodox community!

Overcome by emotion, in a certain lofty sense no longer her own mistress, Pernelle had caught the hand of her poor kinsman. Without false shame, equally free from parade, she now spoke out—

'Reverend sir,' she said, inclining herself before the pastor, 'join our hands, bless us by the way. I, the Catholic Pernelle, wed my kinsman, the Protestant Laurent. So in the future may our alien faiths be reconciled!'

'Amen!' cried a deep bass from the crowd.

Pernelle recognised the armourer's voice. His word was caught up by those around. A few, a very few, crossed themselves and looked askance. The rest yielded to the movingness of the scene. Some sobbed, some fell on their knees in prayer, others thanked God aloud. And a yet heartier Amen found echo far and near, when with unsteady hand the pastor in faltering tones called down a blessing on the pair.

Just then the hammer-man in the clouds struck the hour of noon, raising his arm, so beholders fancied, with alerter swing, adding sonorousness to each beat. And hardly had the Fleming finished his task than all the church bells of the city rang out in merry peal, these too, it seemed, twice as far-sounding and jubilant as of old. East and west, north and south, that inspiriting carillon reached. The bargeman and tower heard it by the crystal-clear, soft-flowing Ouche, the husbandman caught the sound as he weeded his young corn on the plain looking towards Langres, the vine-dresser paused to listen on the Golden Hills. And each nodded his head, murmuring over his work, ' The passing of the deputies! Ah, well-a-day!'

To these sweaters for a crust of black bread, the event seemed impersonal; their hard lot could hardly be bettered even by the States General!

CHAPTER VIII

A MAIDEN WOOER

AFTER the piled-up excitements of such a day, an interview and final understanding with Laurent seemed a bagatelle. In that light Pernelle regarded it, but to the young man things came differently. Personal dilemma of cruellest kind occupied the first place in his thoughts. The summoning of the States General, the coming struggle on behalf of the people, the mooted reformation of laws and government, were lost sight of, dwarfed to insignificance. He could only think of the childishly trusting heart he was destined to break. Yield to Pernelle's super-royal generosities, and Finette would be solitary as himself, only without a stinging conscience. Accept vagabondage, a life of shifts, perhaps hunger and nakedness, and she must weep uncomforted all the same. The leading incident of the day, so he felt sure, friends and neighbours regarded Pernelle's initiative, but doubled, tripled his difficulties. To refuse the hand held out to him after what had just happened, were surely an affectation of contempt, a slight not only on the chivalrous girl, but upon her sex. Could chivalrous feeling, indeed, go farther? Opulent, high-spirited, fair to look on, Pernelle, in popular phrase, might marry any one. Even the Fleming would descend from his airy perch at her bidding, the gossips said. It was well known that half-a-dozen prosperous citizens had courted her in vain. And she was to be flouted by her own fosterling, a poor apprentice, whose father had been branded, pilloried, imprisoned; whose grandfather had been chained to the king's galleys; who till a year ago had himself no right to bear their name, being Protestant, and as such illegitimate in the eyes of the law!

Whilst the young man thus feverishly awaited an explanation, in Pernelle's mind the coming confidence aroused no flutter. A confidence, indeed, she hardly regarded it. To his dismay, on being summoned to his mistress's presence, he found the armourer by, folks going in and out, the bright little salon with alcoved bed, scene of a levee.

'Welcome, Laurent,' Pernelle said, in a tone that was not of yesterday. His new position had altered everything, and not in her own eyes only. As neighbours came and went, the favoured suitor received approving looks and flattering innuendoes. The poor apprentice had become a personage. One or two even ventured on a congratulation, but Pernelle cut them short. She could only think of her uncle and his mission.

'Welcome, Laurent,' she repeated, adding, as she took his hand and placed it in that of the armourer, 'Wish the representative of the people God-speed.'

'Tut, tut, good wishes will keep,' replied Parfait, with a shrug of the shoulders; 'although,' he went on, 'who knows when the opportunity will come to either of us again?'

Laurent, hat in hand, eyes fixed on the ground, stammered out a complimentary word.

'I understand all that you would say. My own thoughts you may not so easily get at,' Nesmond continued. Holding the other's arm, he added with emphasis, 'Hearken, boy.

Hitherto your case has been a hard one. No fault of your own made you penniless and a hireling. I suppose I pass for a godless man, but my creed is this: we were sent into the world each to do his work bravely and honestly, not to waste time over matters beyond the grasp of the wisest. There are principles I would die for, as well as any man; for a figment of imagination, never! Let these things be. You were right to follow in the footmarks of a worthy sire. And to-day you harvest your reward.'

He glanced from the serene figure in white, to the shrinking, as he supposed overjoyed, lover.

'You wished me well of my new dignity just now. What shall I say to the winner of such a bride?'

Pernelle was too much occupied with other thoughts to heed the remark. In fancy she followed the deputies on their way, forecasting their arrival in Paris, dwelling on the great tasks awaiting them there. Oh, to be by, to exchange the counter and the gossiping of a provincial town for the larger, enlarging life of the capital! Even Laurent's smothered remonstrance and appealing look did not attract her notice.

'You have done your kinswoman credit so far,' resumed the armourer, 'neither shaming her by word nor deed, repaying as far as lay in your power her beneficence to you and yours. The time has come when you will be able to discharge a twofold debt. As head of a house, protector of minors, upholder of an honoured name'—

'Hear me,' the young man cried, his face aflame, his eyes glistening. 'Sir, my cousin, I am not worthy.'

'Modesty to-day is in its proper place,' Parfait said, rising. 'To-morrow, unless I misread the times, men will need other qualities. Niece, you have done well. Laurent's self-depreciation is his best advocate'—

'You do not understand me,' Laurent broke in desperately.

'Ah! here I am an interloper. Such explanations are matters for two,' was the smiling reply. 'But I must be off. Niece—and nephew'—

'Hear me!' again put in the young man.

'Niece and nephew—my blessing,' the

armourer retorted hastily. Pernelle accompanied her uncle to the door, the pair embraced each other without a word, then she came back flushed and tearful.

The glow of enthusiasm faded as she reseated herself beside her lover; she became the Pernelle of common days. Generous, even magnanimous, but eminently practical, devoid alike of sentimentality and pettiness, her judgment as unerring in weighty affairs as in selecting silks and laces, Pernelle's deepest feeling hitherto had not taken the form of romance. She gave a little sigh as she sat down, but it was no sigh that belonged to the fireside or a lover. The yearning was for graver subjects that had to be put aside, betrothal, contracts, and wedlock taking their place.

'I have for some time made up my mind to marry,' she began, frankly and deliberately as if she were speaking of a commercial partnership. 'A house like mine requires master as well as mistress. You are gentle but resolute. I feel sure that you would enforce your authority over my sisters and serving-people. I should be freer, too, to make those journeys to Paris and Lyons so necessary to one of my trade, the business would be furthered. But it is your own interest I have most at heart. My mother's family is very dear to me. Our marriage contract shall testify to my confidence and affection.'

Collected as before, she rose, and, unlocking her escritoire, took out a notary's deed, Laurent watching every movement with the look of one whose will is paralysed.

Quite calmly, and standing by the window near him, she began to read. The long twilight of early summer had not yet faded. Fair indeed the view from this side casement, the graceful pinnacles of Nôtre Dame pencilled in silvery grey against a belt of pale amber sky, one by one, stars glimmering faintly through the blue above. Immediately about the mercer's shop all was hushed; from afar came the noise of revelry and rejoicing, music, dancing, and illumination in honour of the great day.

Amid the peace and beauty around, Laurent felt close shut in prison, no door of escape within reach. The sound of Pernelle's clear, measured tones roused him. He jumped up and placed an imploring hand on the parchment.

'Pernelle, my cousin,' he cried, 'this marriage cannot be!'

Wholly misconceiving both word and action, the generous girl held fast to her document, and, with a little murmur of impatience, went on.

'Forgive me for appearing headstrong,' she said with charming candour. 'You have ever been too humble, my poor Laurent; you seem to think the ruin incurred by your family a disgrace—it is instead an honour'—

A ray of noble emotion lighted up her face, her voice trembled.

'My suitors up till now have offered me common things, prosperous circumstance, good repute, and the like. In you I recognise, not the scapegoat of fortune, but the hero.'

'If I were! Heroism would stand me in good stead now,' the young man said, laughing bitterly. 'Pernelle, your generosity is wasted—not on a renegade to his faith—Heaven forbid!—but to his duty. I have deceived you.'

Pernelle let the vellum fall; she moved away from him.

'You have formed some disgraceful connection?' she asked haughtily.

'Disgraceful in the eyes of the world, but honest before Heaven,' he went on, now speaking out. 'For a year or more I have been betrothed to one luckless as myself; our very misfortunes bringing us together.'

He waited, hoping that she would divine the rest. Pernelle, looking straight at him, demanded his whole story.

'I speak of Finette,' he said very quietly. The painfulness of the interview had taken all the courage out of him, he could only endure to the end in passiveness.

Pernelle was given neither to haste nor excitement. She deliberated for an instant, then replied with a touch of scorn—

'You promise marriage to a peasant girl, and in my service, without a word to me? But wrong-doing brings its own penalty. To-day's compact is not to be broken.'

'We love each other,' Laurent murmured; had he murder on his conscience he could hardly have looked guiltier.

'Love?' Pernelle exclaimed, not indignantly, still less unkindly, voice and look expressed amazement and contempt only. ' You can speak of love under such circumstances and at such a time? But it is now too late to think of yourselves.'

Pride not permitting allusion to the morning's event, giving him time to recall it, she added—

'A girlish fancy is easily forgotten. Finette shall be consoled with a little dowry, and wed an honest vine-dresser. You cannot make a laughing-stock of your cousin's name.'

Every word, every turn this explanation was taking, made his case more desperate. How could he prove his loyalty to Finette without playing the traitor to his good genius, his benefactress? Pernelle, he knew, could endure slights, ingratitude, even bad faith. Feminine pride and high spirit could not brook the scoff of the world and contempt of the vulgar.

'Let us say no more,' she added, rising and putting away the deed. 'That poor child, as I say, shall be provided for, her name shall never prove a subject of contention between us. Years hence you will thank me for this interference, for having pointed the way to honour and fortune.'

She made for the door, dismissing him by a

sign. He caught her hand, kissing it with ardent yet most unloverlike appeal.

'Oh, my cousin,' he said, 'you are great and generous. You must understand, pity, pardon me. I cannot give up Finette. Our love for each other has grown with the years. The fortune you speak of would be purchased at cost of a broken heart.'

'Good names are lightly dishonoured, hearts not so easily broken,' was the proud reply. 'As you will, then. No necessity for a word more.'

Without the usual kind greeting, without a compassionating look, she opened the door, and he passed through the dusky, deserted shop into the street.

CHAPTER IX

CURÉ, SEIGNEUR, AND PROLETAIRE

WHILST the townsfolk were holding revel, a tatterdemalion party of three supped gaily in honour of the event.

Before the city gates closed, Fortuné was well on his way home. Home, in the full acceptation of the word, he had none, but as his namesake of the field, he contrived to find bed and board from day to day.

The prey of one class was the providence of another—this week's jail-bird, next week's prodigal—and by an irony of fortune, denouncers and protectors were constantly changing sides. Fortuné had long discovered, alternately to his cost and advantage, that self-interest is the mainspring of human action, only fanaticism getting the better of personal ends.

To-night he did not make for the hamlet over against the town. 'Little Finette will have some neighbour to bear her company,' he mused as he glanced that way, then turned in another direction.

No sooner did he find himself clear of the patrol, than away went infirmities one by one. Crooked knees, bent shoulders, palsied hands, and sightless orbs were made whole in a trice. Briskly as gallant keeping rendezvous, he stepped out under the rising moon. An hour's unbroken march brought him to one of those white-walled, grey-roofed villages, counterpart of many between Dijon and the Plat de Langres, so strikingly contrasted with their neighbours of the Golden Hills. Just now what natural beauty lay around the tumbledown manor whither he directed his steps was obscured; only sharp contrasts of light and shadow indicated patches of corn and fallow, with alternating bits of forest and thicket. The château, as this dilapidated old building was called, must at one time have possessed great treasure, so enormous the walls enclosing it on all sides. Towards the sun windows looked liberally, but at the back neither light nor wayfarer could effect easy entrance.

Stealthy as had been Fortuné's movements

in the city and suburban villages, he now knocked at the postern boldly, the dogs in the courtyard making friendly little noises as he called each by name. A minute later, and two figures, almost as tatterdemalion in appearance as himself, opened the door.

The bearer of the lantern, and evidently master of the house, wore a grotesque costume, half aristocratic, half proletarian, alike long-lappeted vest of richest brocade, and bourgeois riding coat of sober hue, being weather-stained and threadbare; his *jabot* or frilled shirt-front of fine lawn delicately embroidered, was yellow and tattered; still more incongruous were the silver shoe-buckles with coronet and monogram surmounting rusty black stockings and worn-out shoes.

His companion in clerical garb was even worse clad. The faded, frayed soutane told a pitiable tale of penury and neglect.

Neither man owed nature any grudge. Just past middle age, with French regularity of feature and symmetry of limb, hair slightly grizzled, skin brown as that of sea-farers, white teeth, all the whiter by such contrast, they would both have delighted a portrait painter.

Gaiety under drawbacks, the *ancien régime* consoling itself, were here aptly illustrated. Fortuné himself did not readier forget lifelong ills in a whiff of good fortune than these two.

'I've news for you, Monsieur le Marquis, such news!' Fortuné cried, rubbing his hands.

'Our stomachs await you more impatiently than our ears.'

'A moment,' Fortuné exclaimed. 'Truly a wonderful day for rich and poor! Huguette'—

'Your wallet, I say, first, and your good tidings afterwards,' said the host.

'Did you ever hear the like? As if houses and lands escheated even to a noble marquis every day?' put in the smuggler, glancing from host to fellow-guest. 'I tell you, Monsieur le Marquis, Huguette is dead, you may now claim your own.'

'An acre of land'—

'Well-nigh two,' interrupted Fortuné.

'And a mud-built cabin; as far as I am concerned, the crone might have given them to the first comer. But now'—

'Money the poor soul had none, and her cow died in the spring, as perhaps you know,' added the other, with a sly look.

'Leave Huguette alone and come inside, I tell you,' reiterated the marquis. Then he bolted the door, set down his lantern, and with extraordinary nimbleness the pretended beggar was searched from head to foot, a mere shadow remaining; the solid figure was reduced by a third. First a pasty was brought out, next a bottle of wine, these carefully packed in his wallet had done duty as a hump whilst on his rounds; next, the uproarious searchers laid hands on smaller, more compressible objects, dried fish neatly rolled, tiny packets of coffee and tobacco, a precious little lump of sugar wrapped in gauze paper, each discovery evoking a chorus of approval.

'You see, Monsieur le Marquis, Father Albin, Renard is as good as his word,' Fortuné said, wiping his beaded forehead, 'you have both saved him from the trap many a time. I am not ungrateful. And to-day the rogue has turned honest fellow! No need for smuggling or pilfering! Lord love you! the townsfolk are so head over ears in love with their States General, I could have had even the Jacquemart from Nôtre Dame for the asking.'

His hosts seemed hardly listening, so busy

were both with their unpacking and gathering together. Crossing the courtyard, they ascended an outer stone staircase leading to an enormous room, bare save for chairs, table, dog-irons, large buffet and coffer in carved oak. Preparations for supper had not got beyond the placing of knives, forks, and plates; but in a wicker basket close by stood a ring-shaped loaf of coarse rye bread about the size of a carriage wheel.

In less than a quarter of an hour the trio sat down, blazing wood fire and tallow candles animating the scene. Under the table, patiently but confidently awaiting their share of the feast, lay three huge dogs.

'Come, Renard,' said the marquis, when the pasty was demolished, and the generous wine had begun to make the facial muscles curl upwards. 'Now, tell us what happened to-day.'

He looked ruefully at his own garments, next at the curé's, adding—

'Father Albin and myself had our own reasons for staying away. Sapristi!' he cried, smiting his coat lappet with dismay—he had just discerned a new rent; 'imp of darkness, at your tricks again!' then good-naturedly as before he resumed. 'You know that the Dijonnais would sell his soul for a fine show or a gingerbread any day. But the States General—what said folks—that the like of us would be a whit the better?'

That last phrase, 'the like of us,' seemed no mere figure of speech. The Marquis de Velours, who could count his regulation titles of nobility, and whose ancestry dated from the Crusades, might have passed for a second Fortuné, one pariah of society more. As in the other's case—the protégé of one day was the providence of another—dire encounters with poverty, sordid dealings with others more wretched than himself, had neither dulled his wit nor blunted his moral instincts. A man is, however, what his entourage makes him. The naturally fine gentleman was only at his ease among boors and rustics. As to Father Albin, the parish priest, his condition also only just raised him above want and vagrancy. He had a roof over his head, it is true, and a position recognised by the law and society. But no less alertly than the marquis could he accept a beggar's banquet, largess of weightier services. To both, Fortuné had more than once owed his life, let alone limbs and liberty. In their turn, they were indebted for many a poached or smuggled treat, fish and game from preserves of richer neighbours, salt, tobacco, brandy from the king's customs, a dozen necessaries not to be honestly bought.

'You gentlemen say your say. I'll have mine as soon as the table is a bit lighter,' said the poacher slyly, and with affectionate glances at cup and platter. 'When a good meal comes only once in a way, we must take care to fill every corner.'

The marquis leaned back meditatively. Was there inherited fastidiousness in that gentle, yet half disdainful pushing away of unemptied glass, that careless rejection of crowning dainty, some feeling of shame amid this squalid fellowship?

'The like of us or the like of any others?' he began. 'What good can States General do France and Frenchmen now? How say you, reverend father? To my thinking, the sooner an earthquake or universal deluge swallows us all up the better.'

'I have no ears for blasphemies at table,'

the curé replied, helping himself to the dish opposite. 'When our good friend and I have cleared up everything, then, Monsieur le Marquis, have a care!'

The threat was flung back jestingly. 'We are all drowning rats, and may abuse each other as we please. A pretty confessor indeed! Hand and glove with poachers and highwaymen!—no offence, my good Fortuné. But now tell us, what said the townsfolk?'

'Excuse me, you gentlemen say your say; I will listen a few minutes longer,' Fortuné replied, casting rueful glances at the curé, as for a wager the pair plied knife and fork.

'What can the States General do for one in my case?' continued the marquis; 'and one of hundreds—noble without fortune, seigneur without lands, gentleman without bread to eat, hardly the wherewithal to cover his nakedness! Just look at yonder coffer, it is cramful of title-deeds as a graveyard full of bones, none of more value to me. How can a poor wretch pay the seigneur his dues when he has neither corn to grind, wine to measure out, poultry at his barn door? As to title-deeds of other kind, they dwindled to nothing long ago.

Ah, I forget the great news I have just heard.'

He patted Fortuné on the shoulder, adding ironically—

'To nothing? What am I thinking of? Did I not five minutes ago inherit an acre of land— no, was it an acre and quarter?—mud hovel and how many lean hens, did you say? the Marquis de Velours, being heir-at-law of Dame Huguette, a widow without children, and as such having no power to will away her plot of ground, originally purchased from my family. My grandfather came straight from Versailles, from the service of the Great King, a ruined man. The court had swallowed up everything, fortune, honour, decorum. Even the peasants were better off, they contrived to buy his last remnant of land. What, I ask, are the States General going to do for me? Restore the millions squandered on court ceremonials or raising soldiers for insensate wars, piece together my dismembered estate, repair the havoc of generations? Things have long been past patching up, I tell you, and there is nothing for us all but a second deluge.'

Fortuné crossed himself and looked at his

neighbour. The curé, without appearing to notice the last sentence, now broke in.

'The court, the court! Of course Monsieur le Marquis may be right as far as he goes. For my part, I hold that France has been brought to bankruptcy by overmuch religion.'

'The end of the world can't be far off—hearken to him!' ejaculated the marquis.

Feeding the dogs with one hand, his chin resting on the other, Fortuné now listened intently.

'I say it boldly, overmuch religion has ruined the country. The Church should sometimes act like a poor curé—turn a blind eye and a deaf ear to his parishioners' little slips, pretend not to see or hear this, that, and the other.'

'There is something in that, eh, Fortuné?' interrupted the marquis.

'I am proud to own the fact, no one relishes a heretic less than myself, be it Huguenot, Jew, or Turk. But, parbleu! in matters of religion, men are all like the other sex'—

'Come, come, what do you know about the ladies? For shame!' laughed his host.

Father Albin felt that he could here plume himself on his learning.

'Books teach us what women are as well as life, and I have read La Bruyère. But every fool knows one thing—a woman will sooner suffer herself to be flung into a horse-pond than eat her own words. Thus is it with heretics. Not, perhaps, that they care so very much for their Calvin, their Moses, their Mohammed, but they do care about being able to go where they please o' Sundays. Take myself: I am no better Catholic than my neighbours, but, I hope, no worse. Would I not sooner forfeit my tongue than swear by Luther or Calvin? Well, what has France gained by being religious overmuch, looking to men's souls rather than their bodies? I come from the Cévennes, a region devastated as by Attila and his hosts. Whither went the money of the driven-out Huguenots, their industries, their sons? To enrich other lands, swell the armies of our foes. No; damnable heresies have been and will ever be. Leave them to God, say I. Hell is surely deep enough, eternity long enough, for the worst infidel going, say I. No Revocations, no dragonades for me.'

Warming with his subject, the speaker went on—

'France is religious overmuch but on certain points, in places only. You spoke of your feudal rights just now, Monsieur le Marquis, and what are a poor priest's tithes and dues nowadays but so much make-belief? How can I obtain my tenth of corn when the peasant's harvest is zero? Even the best of us are made to appear as his enemy. This honest fellow knows'—here he pointed to Fortuné—'that but for him I should as often as not fare on dry bread. Yet the Church is richer than the king himself, the Church is fat unto bursting, while her hirelings starve. And those in authority over us, the wearers of mitre and purple, shame us no less by their lives than their revenues.'

'What says my pious Fortuné to such sentiments?' said the marquis, his well-shaped, sunburnt hand, on which glittered a magnificent emerald and diamond ring, toying with his glass as he spoke.

'It is not for an ignoramus like myself to contradict a noble marquis or reverend father,' was the alert reply; 'still, if you wish for my poor opinion, I am ready to give it.'

The host nodded encouragingly, the priest

patted him on the shoulder. Proud to have such listeners, Fortuné held up his head and began.

'If decency permitted, and I could strip myself stark as Adam, I need not so much as open my lips.'

'We won't trouble you to do that,' laughingly put in the marquis. 'Proceed, then.'

'I know nothing of former times or other provinces except by hearsay,' he continued; 'but cannot an ass number his stripes and kicks? Now, I've had too many, and it seems to me that the law wants mending even more than the court and the Church.'

'On my word, the fellow has a head on his shoulders—eh, father? But go on.'

'Why have I been branded with hot irons, flogged within an inch of my life, thrown into dungeons, fed with worm-eaten bread? For heresy, murder, high treason? Not at all. Merely for snaring a rabbit, secreting a handful of salt, giving the bailiff and the exciseman the slip now and then. I'm for punishing the wicked; and if there is only one true religion, then, say I, rack, hang, burn, get folks to Abraham's bosom somehow. But a poor poacher or smuggler is pilloried, imprisoned, tortured, as if he had denied the Blessed Virgin and the saints! No, no; not law but tyranny that. Then, again, far be it from me to speak for myself alone; there is the peasant, he must bury his louis d'or, his Sunday breeches, his flitch of bacon, or the tax-gatherer pounces upon all. Only the rich can buy justice, only the noble's skin is safe.'

'There is a spokesman for the States General —eh, father?' again the marquis broke in.

'What I say is this,' added Fortuné: 'according to my poor judgment, the law, like a good mother, should treat all her children alike, not dole out favours and blessings to some, blows and curses to others.'

'One thing is quite clear, we ought all three to sit in the States General,' replied the other. 'But now tell us, how passed the great day? What said the townsfolk?'

'Little good of their betters,' Fortuné replied, glancing slyly from noble to priest. 'I'm thinking, Monsieur le Marquis, that these elections mean more than men dream of. Dijon, anyhow, has gone mad. But I might keep my tongue hard at work till this time tomorrow, you would not be much the wiser.'

A few minutes later, both curé and poacher were nodding in their arm-chairs; only the marquis seemed further from drowsiness than ever. To and fro he walked gently, careful not to disturb the sleepers, now glancing at the moonlit landscape, once ancestral domain, now at the family portraits around, sadly, forebodingly contrasting their fortunes with his own.

Fortuné's words rang in his ears. Little good of their betters, had said the people at Dijon. But would indignation long remain a matter of words? When alike pen and tongue should become free, and the humblest should dare to set forth his wrongs, what then? How would it fare with himself and his class? On his own conscience lay no burden of oppression. He said to himself, as he cast up the reckoning, he could not have played the tyrant had he coveted such a part. The lavishness and parade of his ancestors had rendered him almost harmless, some kind of consolation at such moments. Little good of their betters! Turning from portrait to portrait, reviewing the careers of each forerunner, he wondered if indeed the day of retribution had come at last, if on his own head must fall accumulated expiation.

CHAPTER X

MARQUIS AND MILLINER

For weeks and months, nay, years, no woman had set foot in the once sumptuous Château de Velours. Hardly, indeed, could the least fastidious feminine soul have put up with such accumulated dust and disorder. The once numerous retinue of former owners was now reduced to a deaf and dumb gravedigger, who attended daily to sweep, cook, and wash. From salon to mansarde, roof to basement, spiders reigned supreme, their delicate lacework veiling faded arras and washed-out panels. Here and there floor and ceiling showed clumsy botches, that was all. The crazy timbers creaked under every footstep; an April shower sufficed to drench the upper storey; whilst worn-out gilded upholstery recalled a rummage sale of bric-a-brac. What rendered the whole so pathetic, was the suggestion of former splendour and arrogance. *Fleur de lis* could be traced on each threadbare cushion, handiwork of noble ladies; quarterings and heraldic devices adorned furniture, plate, and even kitchen utensils. And what did these haughty insignia mean now? To their inheritor a double degradation. The seigneur might starve amid empty titles of honour, such indeed had they been hitherto regarded. He durst not assert his dignity, his true manhood, by work.

Next morning, Velours, as he was generally called, began the day by cleaning his gun. Little in the way of game tempted either to field or forest, but a poor seigneur found himself much in the position of a Red Indian or Pacific islander. He must fish, hunt, shoot, or go without dinner. Moreover, the usual round was an occupation. He could not thumb his favourite Rabelais, chat with his fingers to Maurice, teach his dogs, all day long.

In an ancestral dressing-gown, originally a magnificent garment worn at Versailles, his feet thrust in slippers that also looked an inheritance, the marquis began to clean his gun. On one hand still glittered that splendid ring, gift of Sultan to Crusader of his own name and blood, last relic of former greatness. Not for bread, he declared, not for liberty, not for life, would he pawn Saladin's ring.

On a sudden he heard noises outside, wheels rattling, dogs barking, strangers asking for him, and—could he believe his ears?—a girl reiterating, 'Monsieur le Marquis, can I see him on important business?'

'A woman—a lady, as I live!' muttered the marquis. 'Heavens bless us and save us! is the world coming to an end?'

The decay of noble families in France had brought about one desirable reformation. Vice is costly, the whims of disreputable beauty are ruinous. Born into poverty, descendant of courtiers, spendthrifts, and idlers, for his own career Velours need not blush. An honest woman might at any time cross his threshold without shame. He was thinking now rather of vestments than morals, of tattered brocade rather than rents to be found in his character. But ere he could escape, rustling skirts, tapping heels, and perfumed handkerchief heralded feminine presence. The next moment, Maurice, bowing and scraping, ushered in a young, handsome, and perfectly dressed bourgeoise, of whom he seemed to have some recollection. Surely he had seen that exquisitely neat figure and uncommon face, heard that quick, decided voice before? Of his visitor's rank there could be no question; only young women of the middle and lower ranks ever went abroad and paid visits unattended. But beauty does not depend upon armorial bearings, nor a Frenchman's gallantry upon the condition of his purse. The vision dazzled all the more because it was unprecedented, and quick as lightning came the sense of contrast. Humiliated, out of countenance, all that the luckless host could do was to turn his back to the light as servitor and guest passed into the salon, Maurice most inconsiderately throwing back the shutters.

'Monsieur le Marquis,' began the young milliner in the direct, unhesitating tones of the woman of business, 'I have taken a great liberty.'

'Not at all. Do me the honour to be seated,' he said, placing a chair, immediately and with deepened colour exchanging it for another. The first was unsteady on its legs.

'A thousand maledictions!' he muttered between his teeth, as the back of the second gave way. 'Pray take the sofa.' That at least must be safe, he thought, not without some faint apprehension. What if a rat should frighten his visitor? or, worse still, that slender, exquisitely shod and stockinged foot become the see-saw of playful mice? The lonely man made friends of such little creatures, no poorer and certainly more contented than himself.

The tables were now turned: on the seigneur's side, discomposure, diffidence, even embarrassment; on the tradeswoman's, ease, readiness, self-assertion.

Velours felt a glow of shame as he stood in the clear, penetrating, unevasive light of May. That ancestral gown of once rich violet brocade, the last lustre of silk worn off, the last vestige of original colour gone, mortified as an insult, an arraignment of family history. The dilapidation around but too well became his own shabby figure.

'Permit me,' he said, closing the shutters with impatient gesture; he could no longer endure such tell-tale glare. Then, still standing, he looked towards the intruder for explanation.

Pernelle, meantime, was gradually losing

collectedness. At first, nothing had seemed easier than to do here what she was doing every day, coolly broach a business transaction, blurt out the words, ' Sir, I have come to buy. Here is my money; name your price, please, for so many louis d'or forthwith counted.'

Had she found a normal, or at least traditional, order of things, supercilious lacqueys, long delayed audience in anteroom, off-hand steward or bailiff, passing glimpse of state and splendour, all would have been straightforward. Against impertinent underlings, grasping bargainers, she was well able to hold her own.

The complete disillusion put her out of countenance. Largely endowed with tact, still more liberally with good feeling, she now felt utterly at a loss. The bare mention of crown pieces seemed difficult, the suggestion of immediate payment impossible.

'My name, Monsieur le Marquis,' she began apologetically, 'is Nesmond. I believe I have had the honour of seeing you in my haberdasher's shop.'

'True, true,' he replied, now recognising in his visitor the Beautiful Mercer of Dijon, recalling certain purchases — they were rare indeed—of tags and buttons, under the great Flemish clock.

'I have ventured on this liberty in order to befriend a hapless girl,' she continued, not in the frank, self-assured tone of the tradeswoman, rather with the demureness and timidity of some convent-bred maiden—'to lend a helping hand to an orphan, one of your own people'—

Her hesitation had the effect of reassuring him. Seeing her really distressed, he now sat down, smiling kindly, encouragingly, forgetting the humiliation of a few minutes before, only bent on putting his visitor at her ease.

That genial, courteous smile revealed a feature not sufficiently taken account of in summing up personal beauty. There is a positive expression in certain teeth, a charm wholly irrespective of symmetry or ivory whiteness. Velours' were small, regular, and of beautiful shape; the smile revealing them revealed character, that large, generous, affectionate nature, cast with how many kindred pearls on dunghill.

'On my word, you enlighten my ignorance,' he replied, thinking it better to make a jest of his decayed fortunes. 'I had no idea that I could claim any retainers — except bats and screech-owls. Who may they be?'

Pernelle coloured painfully, not for his sake, but her own. The reputed poverty of this noble gentleman, heir of ancient marquisate, grandson of the Great King's chamberlain, had hitherto simplified matters; she imagined nothing easier than the projected bargain—so much money down for a cabin and plot of ground, escheat according to feudal law. Her host's ragamuffinly appearance and high-bred air, above all, his mingled gaiety and cynicism, made her task seem more and more arduous. Woman as she was, none the less sensitive because her life was devoted to practical matters, she saw through the veil. This affected indifference hid deep humiliation. Irony was but a cloak for wounded pride.

'It is of Huguette's foster-child I speak,' she went on very demurely, every syllable an apology. 'You may have forgotten a foundling whom the good woman reared as her own.'

'Little Finette, one of the many waifs exposed on the seigneury, the rich and puissant lord was bound to adopt! I remember the child well,' replied the poor marquis, smiling ruefully. Yes, it was all over with him. His last gold piece was forfeited. This charming young citizen had come, of course, to beg, and he could not send her away empty-handed. 'How little she guesses the true state of things!' he thought.

But a moment later his musings took a wholly different turn. Instead of being asked to give, he was asked to receive; under the circumstances Pernelle's money wearing the look of alms. He crimsoned as Pernelle got out the rest.

'It occurred to me, Monsieur le Marquis, that perhaps you would sell Huguette's homestead and vineyard. Finette has been for two years in my service, but I am now anxious to provide for her—give her a dowry, in fact.'

She added, without venturing to look up—

'The purchase would be easy to me, as I lately inherited a small legacy, some money I was charged to make charitable use of.'

The marquis making no answer, she continued, 'In any case I offer a thousand apologies for this intrusion. I have the poor child's welfare at heart. The city has many temptations for one so young and inexperienced'—

Whilst Pernelle grew more and more expansive, Velours fell back upon his old cynicism. He longed to gratify his beautiful and generous visitor, but the inborn pride of race was too strong. Nothing in the world would have been welcomer than a handful of louis d'or, the very notion seemed miraculous, veritable interposition of Providence. Yet he held back. Thus to bare his poverty to the world, chaffer his last bit of land, escheat already paid for twice over, was more than his high spirit could bear. A flush accompanied the apparently careless speech.

'Sell?' he cried, delighted to find a way out of his dilemma. 'If the States General perform half that is expected of them, a few months, nay, weeks hence, the word will have no meaning for men in my case. Do you not know that the old state of things is to be abolished? Feudal rights, so say the knowing, are to go, and with them, of a certainty, many wrongs, on which I for one have not fattened—as you perceive.'

He glanced at the broken-down magnificence

around, smiling grimly. Having chosen the dignified part, he could afford to laugh openly at ill fortune. This prosperous, engaging young bourgeoise might think what she pleased of his circumstances, she should have no reason to despise himself.

Pernelle, reticule on arm—he knew so well what gave it weight and roundness—now rose to go.

'I am much obliged to you for receiving me, Monsieur le Marquis,' she said, venturing upon no further allusion to the land. 'I will not detain you a moment longer.'

'You will perhaps thank me for refusing your offer before the year is out,' he replied in the same half-serious, half-bantering tone. 'Why pay handsomely to-day for what may be had as a gift to-morrow?'

She looked at him gravely. How much of conviction lay under this jesting mood? Decorum forbade the question she would fain have put—Does Monsieur le Marquis believe in government by a free parliament, equality before the law, rights of citizenship for all?

He divined her thought.

'Permit me to gather you a few roses; in the meantime, we can discuss the States General and the millennium our representatives are preparing for us,' he said.

Throwing wide the bay window, he invited her to descend the steps leading to the garden, once stately pleasance, designed by a pupil of the famous Lenôtre, now a mere wilderness. The marquis, who was his own gardener, neglected ornamental borders for pot-herbs and fruit trees, but in this adorable region, flowers take care of themselves. As the town-bred girl was handed down, she drew deep breaths and uttered little cries of surprise and pleasure. The whole place smelt of roses, showed a harvest of pink and carmine bloom; whilst beyond, harvest even more luxuriant and no less lovely, were the apple trees, roseate wave upon wave against the still azure heavens.

That handing down, the courtly grasp of finger-tips, the careful freeing of her dainty skirts from straggling briar, formed as new an experience to guest as host. The marquis could not remember when last he had performed these little offices for a lady. Pernelle had never before been treated after such fashion by grand seigneur. The sense of novelty, of a certain legitimate precedent, was agreeable to both. In the presence of this beautiful, intelligent, dignified girl, Velours forgot his faded brocade and worn-out slippers. Pernelle, for her part, was now set at ease by his friendliness and geniality.

'You are doubtless all for innovation,' he began, smiling archly, as with pocket-knife he lopped the finest roses. 'Women are ever the first in movements of this kind, and I daresay'—here he paused for a moment, apparently weighing his words. 'I hear that young ladies nowadays read Montesquieu and Rousseau; you, living in a city, being your own mistress, engaged in the serious business of life, may be of the number. If so, your mind is made up.'

'Can even the unlettered, the most ignorant, help hoping, believing in the States General?' she cried passionately. 'Think of the wretchedness around us, the oppression of the people, the barbarity of our laws!'

Velours, singling out one rose more beautiful than the rest, clipping off thorns, now offered it, unceremoniously, engagingly, as he might have done to a child. The demarcation of rank made such attentions easy. Pernelle thanked him in matter-of-fact tones, although with evident surprise and a slight blush.

'Hoping, yes—believing, no,' he replied. 'Mind, I am no enemy of free parliaments or of new systems. What have I, what have most of us to lose? But France—I speak of our country as no configuration on the map, but as a body politic—France, I say, is rotten to the core. Of little good to hack and hew branches when the trunk is tottering and unsound; down it must come, root and stem, not a fibre left in the ground. This wholesome process applied to a nation—eh? Have you thought of the consequences?'

'There must be sacrifice, of course, sacrifice and suffering,' Pernelle answered. 'In the end, we should surely gain.'

'If we could count upon living at least a hundred years. Do trees attain maturity in a day? The growth of a political system, the regeneration of a country, require generations, cycles. And meantime'—

He was tying the rest of her roses together as he spoke, and paused between each sentence, adjusting this or that particular bloom to his fancy.

'Meantime, it is as well to prepare oneself for the universal deluge, careless whether we sink or swim. You, I feel sure, await the issue with a courageous heart.'

Pernelle could not explain it, but this mingled pleasantry and foreboding saddened her far more than her uncle's sombre predictions.

'I hope I shall do my duty,' she said, turning to go.

The marquis gave her his arm, making his adieux bareheaded as to a great lady.

'On my word,' he mused, when the calêche had moved off, 'I should like nothing better than to turn mercer and help that adorable girl with her needles and pins. We nobles despise an existence devoted to buying and selling—is it not a thousand times more dignified than fattening — or starving — upon privilege?'

'We bourgeois accuse the aristocracy of selfishness, parasitism, exclusiveness—have not the seigneurs been victimised as much as the poor, rendered odious by circumstances for which they are not responsible, degraded by a condition forced upon them?' thought Pernelle.

She drove home very sorrowfully, for the moment Finette and Laurent forgotten, her mind occupied with new problems. That visit to the château had been a revelation.

CHAPTER XI

THE TEMPTATION

Homeless in the rigid sense of the word, Fortuné yet possessed coverts numerous and inaccessible as those of his four-footed namesake. So long as snow lay deep, some comrade harboured him, charcoal-burner, bargeman, or quarrier. Here to-day, off and away to-morrow, the poacher and smuggler was no more to be caught than Will o' the Wisp or Jack o' Lantern. Whilst gamekeeper, exciseman, or soldier were on his track, he remained invisible. During the long Burgundian summer, he was independent of hospitality—sheltering woods, wide heavens, the very universe, seemed his own.

Next morning he set off for one of these haunts, and who would not have envied his glorious tramp? High above, proudly and sonorously as if deputed herald of flowers and sunshine, flitted the hoopoe, its crest flashing as a trail of fire, its note penetrating forest depths and echoing through open valley. In the close-set coppice woods, homelier birds welcomed the May, May none the less because the times were evil!

Fortuné knew what paths were safe and how to find his own. Noting signs as he went, he at last reached his destination, a few square feet of open turf amid tangled brushwood and lofty forest trees. Having peered, listened, and assured himself past question that the place was inviolate, untrodden by other footsteps, he divested himself of wallet and coat, and crept forward on hands and knees; under one tree higher than the rest, a tuft of grass that he knew yielded to his touch. Chuckling joyfully, he dug with his fingers into the loosened earth, and drew forth a coarse homeknit stocking full of gold pieces.

'Finette's dowry safe and sound. That comes of praying night and day to the Virgin,' he murmured as he crawled back.

Squatted on the grass, he counted and recounted the louis d'or, first placing them in rows, next in little piles, his eyes kindling, yearning, hungering as he gazed. At one moment they glistened with joy, the next they moistened with tears of despair. 'I was right last night. Did justice exist for the poor in France, Huguette's tiny bit of land and cabin would have been Finette's, the good grandame could have willed them as she pleased; and, who knows, I might then have come in for a coin or two? To think that only rich folks can will away their own, that the substance of all who have no children goes to the seigneur! Ah, Madam Law, as I said last night, it is you who are at the bottom of the mischief! Would I could throttle you, vixen, strumpet, hussy that you are, repay your stripes and bruises in kind!'

More and more wistfully he eyed the glittering temptations, more and more bitter grew his mood.

'Of what use to begrudge poor little Finette the money? I cannot for the life of me steal from her, yet one piece or two might have made Fortuné an honest man! A louis d'or, twenty-four livres, would furnish a pedlar's pack twice over. I have a sharp voice and ready tongue. I could draw folk's money out of their pockets, I know, and in country places the damsels have ever a few sous to spend on ribbon. Money makes money. Pedlars even grow rich—but I cannot steal from Finette.'

Very reluctantly he put back the golden crowns—was it designedly or by accident?—leaving out first one, then two. With these he toyed, now he played at pitch and toss, next he made marbles of them, finally, one was put back and one retained.

'What a joke!' he said to himself, as he grew more cheerful. 'No one, not even the neighbours, suspected Huguette of having a halfpenny! Yet by toiling and moiling, by going naked and hungry, she contrived to save for this fosterling and cheat the tax-gatherer! Humph! What would my gentleman say at sight of yonder stocking?'

The singled-out piece seemed to have more fascination for his own eyes. As he gazed, a new light evidently broke on his mind.

'Services of mine Huguette requited by bite and sup, shelter and hearth work. Yet she must have wished me to repay myself for the last. The coffin now—when do poor folks get coffined at all? They just go to the cold earth in decent shirt or shift. But Huguette ever looked high; I felt that I was humouring her.'

Fortuné had never heard of the famous scholastic dictum, that no proposition be accepted until seventy arguments are brought forward in its favour. Nevertheless, he behaved after the manner of dialecticians, piling evidence upon evidence in support of his theory.

'The hammering together of a few pieces of board, and for such a purpose—what am I thinking of? Better go unpaid till the Judgment Day than take churchyard wages of a neighbour. But, now I think of it, Huguette did owe me a livre or two. The good soul never paid, that I can swear, for the last flagon of oil I procured her; and there was a bag of salt, a rabbit—stolen goods, it is true, but anybody's life is surely worth a louis d'or; who would brave the pillory, the whipping-post, the gibbet, for less? And again, well for you, good mother, that I could not cast up with pen and paper! Who else fetched water for you last winter, when the ponds were frozen from December to March? Then your physic, your ointments and purgations—was it not Fortuné who always doctored you and your cow, bringing myrobalan and St.

Cunigunde's herb to cleanse the blood, hyssop for stomach pains, mallows for winter coughs, dittany to sweat away fevers. But I must leave off, or I shall feel that poor little Finette's dowry belongs to me. I thank you kindly for the louis d'or, Huguette. It is not Fortuné who will forget your soul in purgatory.'

The shining treasure was no sooner put away than he started up. As ejected poison, he now thrust aside the money.

'Spawn of Satan, devil's brood!' he cried, uttering a dozen execrations in a breath. 'Is it thus a poor man's soul is snared by the evil one?'

Falling on his knees, exorcising the tempter with a prayer, he next turned to his birds.

His love of linnets and robins was as the love of children to happier mortals. Driven by hunger, it must also be admitted by taste, to trap wild boar, forest deer, and smaller game, he ever spared these companions of his solitude, digging little reservoirs for their use in dry seasons, planting the wild cherry, enticing them to good fellowship by various devices.

He now imitated first one note, then another, each call bringing a flutter of wings and peering heads. Soon the bower was animated with timid, inquisitive twitterings, each intruder apparently taking counsel of his neighbour.

Prince of woodland, the outcast was now revenged of society. Who in those days of heaviness and apprehension would not have envied such a realm, subjects so artless, scenes so peaceful? Through the gently swayed boughs showed the warm heavens, tablets of blue enamel, as the sun mounted, the upper leafage borrowing the brightness of gold. No one molested him here, no one questioned his right of sovereignty. Only the curious little birds fetched comrades, each saying to the other plainly as voices could speak, 'Who may this be?' A few crumbs, a reiterated invitation, and the chattering company became at home.

Having thus amused himself, he lighted a few chips and cooked his breakfast, next arranged bedstead of branches, mattress of moss and fern, overhead roof of thickly pleached boughs, and drowsed and dawdled away the hours with the patience of an old prisoner. Twilight saw him once more on the march. His heart was light, no bit of gold had been left behind.

When, towards nightfall, he came within sight of St. Bernard's birthplace, he found the place lighted up as for carnival. Arrived midway between road and hill-top, sounds of noisy mirth reached his ears. Folks were evidently singing and dancing round a bonfire. The open space here, bordered with trees, served alike for fairs, markets, religious processions, and homely festivals. His neighbours then were fêting the States General, contributing their part to the universal celebration?

Fortuné relished a gala day as well as any, but he felt the necessity of precaution. With Finette's little dowry fastened to his belt, he was less disposed for prison than ever. The glimpse, therefore, of a vast and very mixed company put him on the alert. Watchmen, patrol, officers of the excise were men with the rest, as ready, when off duty, for a drinking bout, or round with neat-footed damsels. But their eyes would be on him all the same. In order to make assurance doubly sure, no sooner had he reached the outer trees, than, nimbly as a squirrel, he was off the ground and lost to sight amid the boughs of the first that came handy.

To his astonishment, and, at first, dismay, one of the supposed branches laid hold of resented the intrusion, and quickly shifted place. He was not alone even here; some other luckless wight had taken refuge before him.

There could be no mistake, nothing is easier than to distinguish a man's stout ankle from an inanimate bough; moreover, the quick movement spoke for itself.

'Well,' reasoned the new-comer, 'friend or foe, I have the better of him. He cannot get down without disturbing me; but whew! I can be off and half-way down the hill ere his own feet touch the ground.'

Squat as mice the pair kept their places, Fortuné making the best of his position, on the alert for the least sign. After a little his fellow-captive's silence and rigidity reassured him; he now began to peer, listen, and indeed quite enjoy himself.

The scene below was one of extraordinary animation. A tent had been erected for the sale of coarse gingerbread and syrups. Lanterns were hung here and there. In working dress, unaccompanied except by their own voices, old and young now joined hands in Provençal, or the round farandole.

Homely although these revels, they outdid many a princely festival. Thrice happy folks that could thus dance amid sordid care and leaden gloom!

The joyous band did not consist of swains and sweethearts only. Alike white-haired patriarch and toothless grandame footed it merrily, keeping time with the youngest. Many, indeed most, had risen with the sun, bodily weariness was forgotten, home-made liqueurs, plentifully diluted in water, and drunk out of coarse earthen mugs, acted as a stimulant, cakes of honey and buckwheat flour constituted a feast. As night wore on, spirits rose, voices grew higher, laughter more hilarious.

Fortuné's ears soon told him that recent events had lent a new character to this rustic merrymaking. Instead of the usual refrain, folks were singing one new roundelay after another — doggerel, apparently inspired by Huguette's dying words, and the petitions sent up to the States General.

CHAPTER XII

THE CARNIVAL OF THE CAHIERS

So it was, indeed, although the exuberant mirth and warm reception of each ditty suggested benefits rather than wrongs, privilege rather than injustice, as the burden of their song. These ready-witted peasants had not lived for the last few months in vain. Under the self-same trees, the entire community had lately deliberated on the cahiers, or petitions, at that time being drawn up by every town and village throughout France. One white-haired veteran had meekly suggested that the peasant should be allowed to sow his corn without awaiting seigneurial permission. A second honest carle as timidly, perhaps hopelessly, put forward the proposition that every farmer might be his own miller, instead of being obliged to patronise the seigneurial mill. A third speaker, bold Jeanne, Fortuné's visitor of yesterday, declared that if the States General would allow poor folks to have their own bakeoven, for her part she should feel satisfied. A fourth pleaded for free roads, rivers, and markets, abolition of tollbars and bridges. 'Why,' quoth the speaker, 'before I get my corn or pigs even to Is-sur-Tille or Auxonne, I have paid a score of such dues, they have eaten off their heads!' And, of course, one and all joined in the hue and cry against *taille* and *corvée*, arbitrary taxation in general, the hydra-headed feudal system, that made men little better than slaves.

Now Fortuné heard the following—

'Sow, sow, sow, fatten the harvest field,
 Ours to toil and moil, but ours henceforth the yield!'

And now this—

'Grind, grind, grind, millstone belongs to me,
 No seigneur's time to bide, no seigneur's dole as fee!'

A third strophe received even louder acclamation—

'Knead, knead, knead, bundle the faggots in,
 Taxed no more the flames, taxed no more the bin!'

With increasing fervour the fourth was caught up—

'Pack, pack, pack, to market off and away,
Roads and rivers free, not a single toll to pay!'

Popular enthusiasm reached its height when a quatrain was given out summing up the rest—

'Sing, sing, sing, gone the tyrant's day;
Frenchmen will be free, none shall say them nay!
Dance, dance, dance, light of heart and toe;
Good times approach faster than we go!'

The singing and dancing now became almost frenzied. Hand in hand, the homely Bacchanals whirled in widened circle around the bonfire, its flames lighting up kindled eyes and flushed cheeks. There was no coquetry, or what passes by the name, among the young men and maidens; kiss, hand-clasp, embrace, to-night meant something deeper, more magnanimous than courtship, and were shared by all, warm tears relieving overbrimming hearts.

In the midst of this excitement, Fortuné heard a timid, familiar voice underneath his airy perch.

'Oh, Laurent, how you, startled me!' cried Finette. 'I had just come with Douce, the neighbour who has been keeping me company, to see the bonfire and the dancing. But first tell me, what are the folks so pleased about?'

A man's voice, youthful, troubled, but decided, made reply; that also Fortuné recognised.

'The minx has a lover, eh? and, as I live, young Mariol the Huguenot!' said Fortuné to himself. 'He has turned her heretic into the bargain, I'll be bound. All the more reason why I look to her gold pieces!'

Laurent showed loverlike readiness for impersonal talk. Finette's question indeed came as a relief. He laughed a little contemptuously. The whole business, States General, cahiers, and rejoicing, seemed a farce, just then, to this sceptic of twenty-two.

'You remember what I told you about the free assembly summoned in Paris, and the petitions for new laws sent up by the provinces. These poor souls imagine they are going to get everything they have asked for—one law, one taxation for poor and rich, and, to sum up, liberty for all to think as they please. They had better ask for the moon and have done with it!'

Artless little Finette pondered. These problems seemed utterly beyond her.

'What was the show like at Dijon?' she

asked, adding timorously, 'And what did Pernelle say?'

Before Laurent could get out the two or three cruel words revealing all, a sudden uproar diverted their thoughts. Some reveller, less excited and keener of vision than the rest, had caught inkling of the captives, Fortuné squatted below the parting branches, the other higher up, flattened at full length on the trunk, holding fast as best he could with both arms.

'A crow, a crow!' cried the espier triumphantly.

'A crow, a crow!' shouted his companions. Quick as lightning the ring was broken up, one dancer seized a lantern, another a torch; in the twanging of an arrow, the tree was surrounded.

Fortuné seized the stout ankle overhead, muttering good-natured imprecations. 'Dolt of a mother's son that you are, cannot you hitch an inch or two?' he cried; not that he feared his neighbours, but supposing an enemy happened to be among them! He was ever unfortunately wanted by emissary of one law or another, royal, seigneurial, municipal. What if he were dragged to prison now, Finette's dowry taken from him?

'For mercy's sake, give me a heave forward,' answered a doleful voice, 'and just free my soutane.'

Fortuné obeyed, now chuckling as he recognised in the speaker Father Albin. The worthy curé's errand was harmless enough. He could not show himself upon such an occasion, but it was really his duty to see what went on; he must, however, on no account be discovered. The village folks might resent such espionage; and, who could tell? men's spirits were in a ferment, hard things about the clergy, their wealth, their privileges, were passing from hand to mouth; it behoved the humblest ecclesiastic to be prudent.

'Up you go, reverend father,' whispered Fortuné, with a lusty push. 'After all,' he mused, 'priests are men, why should not they join in a little harmless amusement? A lass's ankle now—can the sight of that be sinful?'

Derisive shouts, loud guffaws, rough pleasantries, betokened recognition on the part of the dancers.

'What! were we to have an extra sermon?' shouted one more venturesome than the rest.

'Come, Monsieur le Curé, for once let us teach you a song instead!'

'And you, old foxy!' exclaimed a second, 'why on earth should you take to the tree? you are among friends.'

'Down with you both!' put in a girl, emboldened by example. 'Foot a measure, join in a ditty with us.'

The warmer the invitation, the faster both stuck to their places.

'Another hitch, my good Fortuné; I won't forget this good turn,' whispered the poor priest. 'Ah, some one throws missiles!'

Only a woman's kerchief was tossed up by way of challenging to the dance, but soon followed sand, leaves, twigs, anything folks could lay hands on. All were in teasing, pranksome humour; the very notion of inspiring terror made them doubly mischievous. Two or three athletes now spanned the tree.

'We'll shake off the fruit! look out for windfalls, youngsters!' shouted a brawny charcoal-burner. He had not the slightest intention of harming any one, but the situation was irresistible. No example is more contagious than that of merrymaking at another's expense. Sticks soon rustled amid the branches, pebbles hurtled against the bark, surrender seemed imminent.

Fortuné trembled for his louis-d'or ; any bush, any tree might conceal an enemy. The worthy priest trembled for his parishioners no less than for himself. A week, a day, and everything was changed throughout France. Why, oh, why had he chosen to-night for such espials? What if the poor people were tempted to roughness, perhaps led into crime, by their own confessor and spiritual father?

'Look you, my excellent Fortuné,' he whispered, 'you are one of them; slip down, speak to the neighbours, parley, engage their attention, and meantime I will make good my escape.'

Fortuné murmured assent, but did not stir. The cunning fellow had discovered a cavity in the trunk; feeling about with his hand, assuring himself of its security, he unloosed his money bag and let the treasure fall.

'Come, neighbours,' he cried, now slipping down. 'It was a pulpit I had chosen here, I wanted to preach. Now, listen, listen to words from the grave. Seize your opportunity, reverend father,' he added in an undertone, then once more raising his voice, shouted to the dancers, 'Huguette, the wise woman, the prophetess, this is what she said'—

Small and slight as he was, Fortuné possessed a voice of extraordinary power, not full and deep, but shrill and piercing. The pompousness and solemnity he now put on struck his listeners; for a moment all forgot his companion aloft, attention became centred on the speaker, the most turbulent stood stock still.

'Huguette was near the tomb as I am to you,' he went on; 'death had hold of her with his ice-cold fingers—(do be quick, reverend father, I can't go on speechifying for ever)'—the last sentence was whispered to the poor priest, who, with soutane entangled, still scrambled overhead—'and this is what she said, neighbours: "Whilst I lay here quiet as a babe, Fortuné, I have had visions, not heavenly ones, but earthly. I beheld just now, I behold it still, another kind of world, in which the peasants toil and moil, become fathers and mothers without cursing." (Now's your time, Monsieur le Curé, slip away.) "Horror and darkness are upon the land," said Huguette, "but following after, days such as the like of us have never seen " '—

Just then, as he slowly rolled out the words, some village wag caught sight of the retreating figure behind. His dash forward and uproarious halloo broke the spell. Folks were more inclined for mirth than solemnity. With torn garments, scratched face, and rueful look, Father Albin was brought back. Jeanne laid hold of one hand, her neighbour Douce of the other; despite his remonstrances, he must caracole with the rest.

'Instead of listening to a sermon, we'll teach you a song, no offence, reverend father,' cried the hard-headed, plodding, reputed money-grubbing Jean—he seemed a different being to-night. Room was made for Fortuné, his mind now set at ease as to gendarmes and excisemen. Once more the round was formed. Higher and higher blazed the bonfire, farther and farther echoed the song—

> 'Sing, sing, sing, gone the tyrant's day;
> Frenchmen will be free, none shall say them nay!
> Dance, dance, dance, light of heart and toe;
> Good times come on, faster than we go.'

Few present perhaps deemed the quatrain

a prophecy. None, certes, guessed that they were singing away the old France, acclaiming the new. Vague hopes animated every heart, limited aspirations filled every breast. The most enthusiastic could not realise that an apocalypse of liberty was at hand, changes unparalleled in legend or history.

Song and dance in France have ever been adored by young and old, the fondlings and the stepchildren of fortune. Other passions may be skin deep, this most innocent one is imbibed with mother's milk, becomes as the marrow of French bones.

And to-day even more readily, crushing toil and merciless oppression were forgotten, piled-up, unmerited ills were lost sight of, even the words folks sang became meaningless. The zest of a song consisted in the singing.

Oh, enviable, unmatchable French light-heartedness, all the more precious because innate as perfume to the flower, hue to the butterfly, trill to the bird! Pandora's gift, a thousandfold compensating for the poured-out vials of misfortune—how little do we guess what France, what all humanity, owes her spontaneous, perpetual smile!

CHAPTER XIII

UNDER THE ELMS OF SULLY

HERE and there, the traveller on French soil comes upon a group of noble elms known as 'The Elms of Sully.' These venerable groves do indeed owe their origin to the great minister of the Great King. True to his maxim, tillage and pasturage are the udders of France, whilst neglecting nothing that could advance either, Sully bethought himself of the beautiful. Embellishing the landscape, affording grateful shadow, the groves of the illustrious Huguenot have been alternately dedicated to romance, festival, and religion. Now lovers' vows would be exchanged and village holiday kept under the widespreading branches; and now, with peculiar appropriateness, a little Protestant flock would there meet in worship. Two years before the summoning of the States General, one atrocious clause of the Revocation had yielded to public opinion. Laurent was no longer illegitimate in the eyes of the law; so far a citizen, he could now be legally married, become the father of legally begotten children. There concession ended. He must still meet his brethren, sing psalms, hear expositions of Scripture, under the Elms of Sully, by the wayside, where he could. The rebuilding of demolished churches, the right of public worship, were rigidly forbidden. Boldly confronting their persecutors, the so-called heretics had ever showed timidity towards friends and kindred. Why needlessly wring fond hearts, trouble pious minds, last but not least, shock inrooted prejudices, sin against accepted standards?

Thus it happened that, although openly avowing the paternal creed, Laurent had always been reticent in the matter of religious observances, with his brethren unobtrusively accepting each new privilege. But the air was now full of compromise, every hour seemed portentous of change, one precedent quickly followed another. Timid folks grew daring, brow-beaters of yesterday meek as lambs.

On the first Sunday following the passage

of the deputies, the country-people hereabouts witnessed a strange spectacle, their presence being stranger far. For the first time since the Revocation—doom of France—a great muster of Protestants was announced between Dijon and Is-sur-Tille, the rendezvous being a grove of elms known as the Elms of Sully. No spot could have been more aptly or better chosen. The trees crown a wide, stony, wind-swept plateau several hundred feet above the level of the sea, and commanding a vast perspective, fit emblem of spiritual freedom. Immediately below lay the ancient hamlet of Gemeaux, only its spire visible above the jagged edges of the little promontory; farther in the same direction stretched the Golden Hills, mere pencillings of purple against the pale blue sky; whilst northward, dark masses against the delicate green of young corn indicated the vast forest, long-lapsed fief of the marquisate of Velours.

Two or three years earlier such a gathering would have been punishable by fines, the executioner's whip, fetters, and even mutilation. It was still deemed prudent to avoid symbol and parade. No rudely improvised altar suggested the sacramental feast, no wooden bench did duty for pulpit. Only nature consecrated the temple, chequered sunshine amid green leaves replacing gorgeous ogive; instead of flute and psaltery, the soft breezes of summer; whilst around, no sculptured saints and apostles incited to prayer, but, hardly less worthy of such office, stood the veteran trees that had rejoiced and sheltered generations.

Along the hot dusty road trudged Laurent and Finette. To-day for the first time they were to worship side by side, drink together out of the sacred chalice, and partake of consecrated bread. Behind, having fallen back with neighbours, was the girl's new protectress, Douce, a good woman whom neither toil nor privation had hardened.

'Why do you weep?' cried the young man, with almost asperity in his voice. 'Our fortunes are no worse than they were—before Pernelle offered to give me her name, I mean.'

'Oh, Laurent, you know why I am too happy and too sad,' answered the little thing. 'Once more let me plead, not wholly against myself. By and by, I shall feel proud and thankful that I helped to make a bourgeois, a rich man of you. My own sorrow will gradually lessen'—

She went on with her artless advocacy, but all in vain. The young man turned upon her with a stinging word.

You forget one kind of poverty you would bring upon me,' he said. ' Is not faith in one's self golden treasure?'

He added, now speaking soothingly, ' Look you, Finette, even if I could forget you entirely, no more remember you than if we had never seen each other, this marriage might make my fortune, it could not make me happy. Pernelle stands too high above me. I should always feel her dependent, her servitor. So have done.'

To please him, she wiped her blue eyes and flushed cheeks, smiled and chatted; but he saw that acquiescence hardly meant conviction. Even this rustic, untaught, timid Finette had thoughts he could not read.

The girl was in the exalted frame that makes martyrs of the humblest. Just so infantine, yet heroic, the little Christian slave Blandine, centuries before, her constancy under Roman inquisitors moving the rude Gallic chieftains to wonder and pity. This new religion, the faith she owed Laurent, influenced every action. She felt, too, so grateful for the gift, so anxious to repay him, even at the sacrifice of her own happiness.

On arriving, they found an immense concourse of people already assembled. The breezy plateau presented the appearance of a fair, from end to end crowded with moving masses, townsfolk and peasants, rich and poor, on tip-toe of expectation, agog to see what Huguenot worship was like.

'Who is that fine bourgeoise looking so hard at you both?' asked Douce, rejoining the pair.

The good soul, although a devout Catholic, could no more stay at home than her neighbours.

Laurent and Finette glanced up for a moment, then on the ground, stammering reply. It was Pernelle, who had accepted a seat in some acquaintance's calêche; not to look on idly inquisitive, but to countenance fellow-citizens, till yesterday under the ban, still so sorely maltreated by the law. Here was a good opportunity for fraternal demonstration and approval. Again, the Protestants were suspiciously regarded by certain classes; there were rumours of ruffianly interference, even of organised opposition. And as if the lives of these newly recognised citizens counted for naught, no agents of law or police had been sent to protect them. Whilst, two or three years before, a handful of old men, women, and children thus met together would have been brutally dispersed by dragoons, their prayer-meeting apparently as dangerous to the State as an invading army, not a single soldier was told off for the safety of hundreds when legitimately employed. All the more needful, thought Pernelle, that orderly, reputable folks should show themselves. She wore holiday dress, and, with two portly dames, no less handsomely attired, formed a striking contrast to the Huguenot matrons in their long, hooded, funereal cloaks. Well, indeed, might they wear black. Had not existence been one protracted mourning?

'What can have brought Pernelle here?' Finette asked in a frightened voice.

'Laurent also was greatly agitated. After what had happened, he could not explain his cousin's presence to-day. The true, the generous motive never once occurred to him. That Pernelle should carry forbearance so far as not only to overlook personal affront, but countenance the aggressor, was a piece of magnanimity beyond conception. These naïve lovers lived outside the great, changing, already storm-tossed world in which she had her being. To the Beautiful Mercer, Laurent's rejection of her hand and foolish fancy had become little things.

'Oh,' replied the young man, anxious to set his companion at ease, 'it is Sunday, remember, when all rich folks are abroad. One show does as well as another.'

He was really thinking not of Pernelle, but of the careless, gaping crowd, to whom this solemn occasion was a mere spectacle.

'Pernelle perhaps has something to say to you. Had you not better seek her?' was the timid rejoinder.

In Finette's eyes their patroness was a wholly superior creature, to be courted, done homage to; no princess higher above them. Humility well became apprentice and serving-maid; hauteur equally beseemed the bourgeoise, the great lady.

'Hush, the service begins,' Laurent whispered, uncovering his head and bowing low.

There was no bell to usher in the congregation, no sacristan to marshal pastor and elders to their places. A circle formed, several deep, the children placed first; then, as the minister, wearing austere Calvinistic garb, took up his post, all standing broke forth in song.

That artlessly-worded hymn caught up by young and old, the first French hymn to greet Catholic ears, had marvellous effect. Onlookers, for the most part, were as ignorant about Protestant ritual as about sun-worship or the doctrine of Confucius. Children of orthodox parents were taught to loathe it like paganish idolatry. What indeed must that superstition be like, how abominable and blasphemous, thus held deserving of outlawry, mutilation, the galleys, gibbet, and stake? General astonishment knew no bounds, when a short but fervent prayer was followed by exposition of Scripture and exhortation to faith, hope, charity, and a godly life, all in mother tongue. But it was, above all, the simple sacramental rite that bewildered outsiders. As the communicants, men bareheaded, women meekly looking down, stood around the pastor, and he handed chalice and bread to each, a text accompanied the ceremonial; to the aged and broken-down were spoken words of comfort and upholding, to the young and valiant a message of courage and looking-forward.

'These Protestants, then, they believe in God and Jesus Christ?' murmured one.

'Heretics folks call them? Why, they read the Bible!' quoth another.

'Huguenots, forsooth!' cried a third. 'Well worth hanging, burning, torturing people who pray to Jesus Christ like ourselves!'

The simple yet solemn celebration brought about a tremendous change of opinion. Bravadoes come to hoot and yell, perhaps also to hustle and maltreat, were subdued by the apostolic scene, bigots shamed into respect and pity. Not a rude expression was uttered, not an offensive gesture indulged in. Under the rejoicing sky, amid the beauteous promise of summer, a new feeling thrilled every heart, a new religion dawned upon every mind. Already the ideal of the Revolution, universal brotherhood, seemed within the limits of possibility.

The mere prospect of liberty disfranchised, the dream of concord united!

This poor France was so weary of hatreds and persecutions, civil warfares, domestic feuds! The thoughtful, no matter their convictions, yearned for toleration. Fanaticism had defeated its own ends. With one voice, the country clamoured for compromise, freedom of thought, equality before the law.

The last of the communicants were Laurent and Finette. As if divining the tie that bound them together, apparently interpreting blushes and downcast looks, the pastor made one text serve for both.

'Be kindly affectioned one to another, with brotherly love, in honour preferring one another'—

Finette did not hear the rest. The service, so simple yet moving, every phase appealing to the individual, had more than touched her; it had revealed a new, heroic self, hitherto undreamed of, but no longer to be kept in the background. The very air of France seemed impregnated with heroism just then. Among the humblest and apparently least enthusiastic, self-sacrifice and loftiness of soul shone forth spontaneously. The most commonplace no longer recognised himself. Whilst Laurent was embracing this brother in the faith and that, she stole unobserved to Pernelle.

'Laurent does not guess, Laurent must not know,' she whispered very quickly, as if feeling that each word sealed a compact. 'Since coming here, only just now, I have made up my mind. He shall never lower himself, ruin his prospects, by marrying me '—

Glancing round, making sure that these confidences were safe, she added—

'Douce, my neighbour yonder, has relations a long way off, on the banks of the Saône. They want a girl, she says, to help with the cows. I will hide myself there. Pernelle, mistress, you will forgive us both, will you not?'

'My poor girl,' Pernelle replied coldly, but not unkindly, 'I have other plans of befriending you both. Stay with Douce for the present.'

'Say that Laurent is forgiven,' pleaded the little thing. Of her own happiness she was hardly thinking. 'Do not let me cause his ruin.'

'A man is responsible for his own fortunes.

Laurent having decided thus, neither you nor I have anything to say,' was the haughty reply. 'But I shall not abandon you'—

'Mistress, mistress!' sobbed Finette.

'I repeat, stay for awhile where you are. You shall hear from me.'

And with that rejoinder, Pernelle turned away.

'What was Pernelle talking about just now?' asked Laurent, coming up.

He too had been greatly moved by the morning's event, but things touched him after different fashion. His voice sounded harsh, his manner was rough, to Finette's thinking. Trial, whilst it softened and sweetened her character, hardened his; religion braced him to the fulfilment of duty, it did not render him gentler, more clinging.

'She says that I am to stay with Douce for the present, and that she will not forsake me,' Finette answered, affecting cheerfulness. The rebuff had by no means shaken her determination. Laurent should be saved in spite of himself. Meantime, she must keep her secret.

CHAPTER XIV

'NOT A BAUBLE FOR MOTHER COUNTRY?'

THE Fleming, keeping time above Nôtre Dame with automatic spouse and bantling, looked down upon many a wondrous sight during this wondrous summer of '89. More fortunate than the comparatively Lilliputian folk underneath, the trio in bronze could remain at their post, yet miss nothing that went on, north, south, towards the rising or setting sun. They could watch the daily muster in the Place d'Armes, that graceful horseshoe before the Ducal Palace, whither flocked Dijonnais centuries before, whenever Charles the Bold took an airing. So resplendent the array of the mad Plantagenet, and so agog the populace to behold, that it was the business of two lacqueys to keep off the curious. This was done by laying lustily on their shoulders with ivory staves, the way being kept by fierce archers; once fairly off, the glittering, gorgeous figure flashed by like a meteor, so at least old chronicles tell us. Stranger spectacles by far now took place under the eyes of the hammerman and his fellow-townsmen. Days no longer resembled each other, hardly an hour but something occurred wholly out of the common way, every evening brought portentous news, every week its catastrophe. The world, the world of France, was revolutionised by the very whisper of Revolution!

And all this time the mass of the generous French people was subsisting mainly on hope, on the promise of to-morrow. The peasants grew more hollow-eyed in the cabin, the kine leaner in the field. There were famine-stricken regions, famine-stricken towns anxiously awaiting news from Paris. The States General, a free parliament, the representatives of the people—would these soon bring a plenteous yield, a cheap loaf? No one will ever know how much hunger and nakedness had to do with this great year.

As yet, buying and selling went on busily under the clock; love of finery and of good cheer still actuated the belles and *bon vivants* of the Burgundian capital. Pernelle's stalls were attractive as ever; and from end to end the city savoured of gingerbread, that unrivalled, time-honoured compound of honey and buckwheat invented by Charles the Bold himself. Pernelle and sober-minded folks, however, grew thoughtful; the pitiful looked to their ledgers and daily outlay; need had come for rigid economy and hitherto undreamed-of self-sacrifice. The events in Paris were but precursive of others far wider reaching; universal revolution meant deserted fairs, empty workshops, inanimate counters. Who could say for how long?

Foremost to take magnanimous initiative was the beautiful city of Dijon. Prouder pageants had been witnessed in the crescent before the Ducal Palace, none more moving than to-day's—a roll-call of the charitable, the beneficent. From lauds to vespers, folks were summoned on behalf of the poor. A collection was to be made, jewellery asked for as well as money.

'I don't mind what sister says,' whispered Barbe to Berthe, as the two girls dressed. 'I am *not* going to give my silver thimble to the mother country, as she calls it. What is the mother country to me?'

'Hush!' retorted the more circumspect, worldly-wise Berthe. 'Unless you give something, Pernelle won't let you go to the Place d'Armes at all.'

'Then I'll buy a brass thimble and toss it in for gold.'

Berthe laughed quizzically. 'You forget Pernelle's eyes will be on us. *I* intend to give these.'

Very ostentatiously she produced a pair of old-fashioned gold earrings. Standing before the mirror, gracefully adjusting the pendants, as gracefully removing them from her ears, she went on—

'You seem to forget, too, that all the town will be staring, and that sister Pernelle is sure to reward us handsomely. Just watch me. "Gentlemen," I shall say as I take off the drops, "I am but a child, a young milliner learning her trade. I give all I have, the most precious souvenir of a beloved mother, for whose soul in purgatory I daily offer prayers."'

'Pernelle won't allow you to say that, because

it is not true. The earrings were paid as a bad debt to her, and she gave them to you.'

'Oh, bother!' was the impatient answer. 'How tiresome it is to be perpetually worried about speaking the truth! What can it matter how I came by the trinkets so long as I give them? Well, I must trump up some other story. "Gentlemen," I will say, "what greater proof can I give of my patriotism, my disinterestedness? Verging on womanhood, no less vain than the rest of my sex, I yet relinquish the contents of my jewel-case."'

In the midst of the little scene entered the ubiquitous, the dreaded Pernelle. There was no eluding the vigilance of this terrible guardian.

'Why such lingering in your bedroom?' Pernelle said sharply. 'The shop is open, your soup is ready in the kitchen. Not another minute's delay, I beg.'

'Dear little sister,' cajoled Barbe, the more daring of the twins, 'we were only making up our minds what to give to the Patrie. Just think, Berthe offers her gold earrings!'

Momentarily beguiled, ever seeking figs of thistles and grapes of thorns, Pernelle bent low, she alertly examined the ornaments, once more appraising their value.

'Good girl! We cannot too early appreciate the value of self-sacrifice.'

'Which means,' thought Berthe, 'that sister Pernelle will buy me a new, fashionable pair.'

'And you, Barbe?' Pernelle added, turning to the younger twin, her sister's junior by an hour.

'Won't Berthe's gift suffice for both?' was the reply.

'How like her!' put in Berthe self-approvingly. 'Sister Pernelle, I told her just now that she ought to give her silver thimble.'

Barbe pouted.

'Not a thimble for the Patrie, for your starving fellow country-people?' Pernelle remonstrated.

'And after all, as I said,' Berthe went on, 'it is not as if nobody would be the wiser; every one will praise us. Uncle Parfait is sure to bring us something pretty from Paris, by way of reward'—

Pernelle threw down the gewgaws with a look the minxes understood but too well.

'You may both go to the Place d'Armes,'

she said; 'but I forbid either of you to give anything'; and thereupon she left them.

No time for the usual recrimination and making up; crestfallen, sulky, and vindictive, Berthe and Barbe entered upon the daily routine. When would the time come—ah, when!—for repayment of these injuries? Pernelle had kept the family fortunes together, educated, trained, fostered them, her very benefits seemed so much unkindness.

Very sadly Pernelle set off for the Place d'Armes, bearing her own gift, an heirloom of intrinsic worth and real splendour. It was a massive chain of Peruvian gold, bequeathed by a West Indian trader to some Nesmond years and years before. Pernelle's paternal ancestor had rendered this merchant signal service, of which the chain was to be perpetual reminder.

'Could a better use be put to ill-gotten treasure?' reflected the young mercer. 'Honest as might have been my grandfather's client, his moidores originated in bloodshed and rapine: let the curse be redeemed by blessings of the hungry.'

She forgot her calculating sisters as she

reached the crescent, not as yet gay with the Tricolour, not as yet ringing with the Marseillaise, but animated by a new spirit. Already love of country, patriotism, the sentiment that had slumbered since the days of the Immortal Maid, were revived. Humdrum natures, obscure folks, thrilled at a voice now heard for the first time, the voice that links men together, makes of heterogeneous masses a nation.

In the centre of this elegant amphitheatre, conspicuously raised, was a huge table heaped with glittering objects. At either end soldiers kept guard, whilst, hedging a way for the donors, stood municipal guards in best array. No one had eyes for the uniforms, so different to the tatterdemalion dress of former days, nor for the violet and ermine of provincial authorities, provosts and men of law. Still less cared any spectator to admire the beautiful framework of the picture, Ducal Palace and Tower, St. Michel's cupolas recalling the Italy of its architect, St. Bénigne with its spire bent in perpetual adoration—above all, the deep blue cloudless heaven. People had come to see who gave and what was given.

Pernelle had reasons of her own for performing this duty unobtrusively. She hardly pardoned herself as yet for the impulsive behaviour of a few days ago. Certain neighbours, she knew, severely criticised that open recognition of Protestantism on the occasion of the great muster, whilst kinsfolk and intimates, alike the orthodox and unorthodox, looked askance at a mixed marriage. None, however, could remonstrate; Pernelle's decision of character prevented interference and staved off criticism. But she was a tradeswoman, and as such obliged to conciliate popular opinion. Very demurely, in neatest possible dress, her gold chain swinging from beautifully mittened arm, she was about to enter the enclosure when a voice called her name.

Glancing up, she saw her host of a few days before, now hardly recognisable. The poor marquis, forced to visit Dijon on business, had contrived to look like other people. Why should a ruined seigneur not borrow his neighbour's redingote, even hose, upon occasions? It must be admitted that the loan worked wonders. Pernelle forgot the threadbare dressing-gown, the slippers worn at the heel, the tattered ruffle. She was only sensible of a double charm. To-day, dignity of mien and manner were enhanced by appropriate dress. So deep the gulf dividing noblesse and bourgeoisie, that no etiquette prevented a seigneur from addressing a shopwoman. His greeting, indeed, was but an excuse to look at her. He hardly knew how much and how often Pernelle had been in his thoughts since their interview. Forgetting his poverty, delighted to recognise fellow feeling in one of higher rank, the young mercer bowed low, yet spoke out freely.

'How happy it makes one to give!' she cried, holding up her heavy gold chain—'to see all France bent on succouring the unfortunate!'

Velours looked as one who receives cruel rebuke. Truth to tell, he had come to Dijon in utter ignorance of this patriotic fête. Newspapers were unknown outside city gates; from end to end of rural France, the letter-carrier was unknown also; of what good letter-carriers when most folks could neither read nor write? Even the rich and instructed within a league or two of towns, remained ignorant of what went on there till weeks afterwards.

'For of course you have heard?' Pernelle added. 'To-day we are collecting money and treasure to feed the starving. Thousands are without work and bread at Lyons; in the villages of the Jura, peasants are actually dying of hunger.'

The poor marquis all the time was feeling in his pockets, he knew well enough that they were empty as far as he himself was concerned. The desperate cling to a straw—what if his lendings contained a coin or two?

Whilst he reddened with alternate hope and discomfiture, Pernelle chattered gaily as before. Raising that beautiful hand and wrist, the white skin gleaming like ivory under her black lace mitten, she pointed to the shining trophy. It told its own tale. Gold and silver plate, jewels and pearls, mosaics, even velvets and lace, made a gorgeous pile. And at every moment the pyramid increased. Grandsires and grandames tottered up with little children. Here would lie some stout citizen's gold snuff-box, there some schoolgirl's silver chaplet, each oblation calling forth tremendous applause.

Mistaking her companion's attitude for indecision, thinking perhaps that a seigneur recoiled from a movement so popular, Pernelle added with gentle raillery—

'Not a bauble for the Patrie, Monsieur le Marquis?'

Velours' mortification now amounted to positive anguish. What would he not have given for a louis d'or, a crown-piece, anything in the shape of money? Baubles, forsooth! the girl's playful suggestion stung him as an insult. Had not one trinket gone after another, and of very truth to feed the starving? But for a ring here, a gold buckle there, first a pearl-inlaid miniature-frame, next a fan that had been his mother's, he should himself have starved long ago. Baubles had fed and clothed him for years past.

Pernelle waited, captivatingly importunate. As a girl smiles upon her lover, caresses him with looks, all the more irresistible because they are angelically pure, she smiled upon the unloved, uncaressed man now. He knew nothing of love, this poor marquis, nothing of women, except the knowledge all men pick up eagerly in their youth and would fain afterwards forget. It flashed upon him as a revelation that his life had been contemptible and bereft.

'Not a bauble for the Patrie, Monsieur le Marquis?' repeated Pernelle.

Velours was in that humour when men are ready to fling away fortune, honour, even life, for a woman's smile. Not venturing to give himself time for reflection, so much as an instant's pause, he took off his diamond and emerald ring, that princely gage of affection from Sultan to ancestral Crusader, offered to a Velours hundreds of years before. Glancing back as he went, answering smile by smile, he marched straight to the trophy and threw down his splendid gift. Then, the applause of bystanders unacknowledged, Pernelle's grateful look accepted shyly, he hurried away. The last five minutes had made him in one sense a bankrupt, in another a millionaire!

CHAPTER XV

'THE BASTILLE, THE BASTILLE!'

THIS first summer of Revolution was fiery as men's slumbering passions; whilst, morally speaking, France trembled on a volcano, ready at any moment to vomit flames and destruction, so the solid earth, parched by long drought, baked through and through by a torrid sun, seemed presageful of catastrophe. Already, indeed, famine was abroad, and in its wake followed pestilence, vindictive sense of wrong, murderous instinct of self-preservation. No one knows, none will ever know, what the French peasant suffered under the Great King — god, as his priests called him — and his successors, the serf of the Middle Ages enviable by comparison.

In the fierce July glare, getting shade where they could, Finette set off with Douce and Fortuné for her new home on the Saône. The little man knew the country well, and was able by many a device to shorten the journey, ten leagues as the crow flew, and an unprecedented enterprise to his companions. Only rich women and business women travelled in these days, country folks for the most part being fixtures.

But proud affection lent Finette courage, and Douce was animated by motives equally strong. The good soul had a son employed by kinsfolk in the village to which they were bound. Fortuné had hinted at Huguette's stockingful.

'Look you,' she had said to her husband, the patient, cheery, artless Félix, so well matched with herself, both so contrasted to their hard-headed, worldly-wise neighbours, Pierre and Jeanne, 'Vélours will sell Huguette's vineyard, so folks say. What if little Finette marries our Edmond?'

The pacific fellow nodded assent, but said nothing. One might have supposed from the general taciturnity, that speech, as well as every other necessity of existence, was taxed in rural France. The Revolution indeed accomplished more than history writes of. With an era of well-being, it restored to the peasant his original gaiety, his inborn garrulousness.

Douce had her way, and set out on twofold errand — firstly, to negotiate these bridals; secondly, to sell at St. Jean de Losne or Seurre a pile of linen, spun and woven by herself. To Finette's romance Douce hardly gave a second thought. Edmond was an honest lad, and wanted a wife. Finette possessed a little money, and wanted a steward thereof. Better reasons for marriage could hardly be found.

On the trio trudged, their guide and protector now carrying one bundle, now another, singing, whistling, telling stories by the way. Freedom, good fellowship, hedgerow snack, he needed no more. And he enjoyed the usual sense of triumph, the smuggler's delight at passing contraband goods. From Douce's gay cotton handkerchief protruded coarse felt shoes and well-darned bedgown. Finette's larger package might well be taken for serving-maid's wardrobe; cunningly folded between each garment were the pieces of homespun linen that the king's excise would have rendered profitless. No less carefully concealed round his own person were tiny quantities of soap, sugar, and other luxuries almost unheard of in country places, the secretion of each hitherto punishable by loss of limb, imprisonment, death.

Still more carefully stowed away were Finette's gold pieces, honestly acknowledged hers, yet so hard to surrender. The treasure seemed his own whilst he had it about him.

'Come, my wenches,' he cried, as the blinding noonday beams found them well on their way, 'what say your stomachs to a meal? Mine has been pestering me for an hour or more.'

The glittering, close-serried spires and cupolas of Dijon were soon left far behind, fainter and fainter grew the outline of the Golden Hills. The landscape grew leveller and more monotonous as they advanced, wide spaces of cleared cornland alternating with stretches of stunted pasture, and tiny plots of Indian corn, rye, or potatoes. Few and far between the lean kine afield, or flock of geese, minded by withered hag or weather-beaten, barefooted girl. They followed the canal that shot straight as an arrow from Dijon to St. Jean de Losne, only here and there in the far distance catching sight of a hamlet, clustered brown-tiled, brown-walled houses; above these, the spire of a church with spread-

ing roof, brooding as a bird over its nestlings.
A few walled-in manors, surrounded by wood,
indicated the more prosperous condition of
larger landowners, their class standing midway
betwean serf and seigneur. Only one or two
châteaux were seen throughout the long
journey, these shut in by trees, standing wholly
aloof, thus symbolising the gulf dividing their
owners from the dwellers of thatched, mud-
built, windowless cabins. The violet and
amber silhouette of the Golden Hills grew
paler and paler, but still remained in sight,
cheering the women, making them feel more
at home.

Squatted on the ground, close to the canal,
leaning against the wall, the trio opened their
wallets.

'Is it France as far as we can see?' asked
Finette, gazing around with bewilderment.

'We should have to walk more days than
we have as yet walked hours before reaching
Prussia or Austria,' Fortuné replied, as he
spoke doling out rye bread and soft, strong
cheese, ladled from an earthen jar. 'What are
you thinking of, girl? We are not yet in sight
of the Saône.'

Humiliated, she held her peace. But the wide, to her thinking immeasurable, perspective still remained a mystery. Was it possible that any country could be so large? To Douce, also, the sense of space and remoteness was overwhelming, uncanny. Whilst Finette felt inclined to weep, thinking of the distance that divided her from Laurent, the good housewife began to accuse herself of temerity. Should she ever see Dijon and the curved spire of St. Bénigne again? Fortuné, stimulated by a plentiful meal—quantity to him was of so much more importance than quality—went on enlightening their ignorance in lordly fashion.

'Don't come for book-learning to me,' he began; 'but when a man has eyes, legs, and an understanding, I take it he can make shift without a map of his own country. Look here.'

He bent forward, and with his stick drew in the white, smooth dust a rough but accurate diagram of the France that he knew, his survey including Burgundy and Franche-Comté, the central point being Dijon. Fortuné's stick, indeed, might have instructed many of his betters in the matter of geography.

'I have not been run down to earth like a

fox all these years for nothing,' he continued, pausing to take a mouthful. 'You see where we are, Dijon. Paris and—so folks say—the sea and England lie behind us; before us, the Saône, the Jura, and the highest mountain in the world, Mont Blanc. When on the top, you hear St. Michael and the angels tuning their harps, and the Blessed Virgin scolding her serving-maids. I've even heard say'—

He swallowed a copious draught from the one bottle of wine they carried with them, a still more copious draught of water brought from the Ouche, and added—

'I've even heard say that cherubim and seraphim have fallen out of the windows.'

'Did any mortal ever reach the top, then?' asked Finette breathlessly.

'Of course, child, or how could Fortuné have heard tell of such things,' put in Douce. The smuggler's experience was immense, and his revelations of a piece with this strange journey. Having got so far from home, she felt able to believe anything.

'Once upon a time, not so very long ago either,' replied the oracle, 'a traveller brought down a brace of doves that had flown from heaven. But hark!'

His look of alarm infected the others. All three became squat as mice.

'You hear horses' hoofs, some one galloping?' asked Fortuné.

The two frightened women nodded assent. Quick as lightning, bundles were hidden in the lodge, Finette's dowry handed to Douce, for the hundredth time the vagabond's last will and testament made.

''Tis the king's men after me,' he said, casting a hopeless look around; there was no chance of escape in this wide, treeless plain. Already his pursuer had come in sight, a few minutes more and he should be a prisoner.

'Mind you, my good Douce,' continued Fortuné in a tone of agonised entreaty, 'this gold piece is my very own; my body will be cast into a ditch like a dead dog, but you will say masses for my soul. Make the money go as far as you can; haggle with Father Albin, he is reasonable. Do your very best. And you, little Finette, if you spend a franc or two on masses for Fortuné's soul, the Blessed Virgin will reward you, never fear.'

Both promised their good offices, Finette against her will—not that she begrudged the money, but as a Protestant she no longer believed in redemption purchasable as wares at market.

'They will cruelly use my body, death is not punishment enough for purloining a bag of the king's salt,' he went on. 'I am not trembling about that, I have a stout heart. But purgatory, purgatory! Shorten the term, Douce. Think of twenty, fifty, a hundred, a thousand years in torment!'

The rider now dashed up, and Fortuné, resigned to his fate, confronted him boldly. How many times had he thus nerved himself to the last calamity, how often gone mentally through his fiercest and final trial on earth! He might, indeed, be said to have died again and again.

What was his amazement when, without so much as an inquisitive glance, the horseman merely shouted and galloped on? All three sprang to their feet, staring incredulously, whilst looking back, flinging his words behind him, the figure flattened to the saddle, increasing his speed. 'The Bastille, the Bastille!' They heard no more, and the words conveyed but little meaning.

Fortuné and his companions little guessed that they were already ringing throughout Europe, knelling doom, announcing mighty advent. The day before had been one of the great days of the world. The Bastille had fallen!

CHAPTER XVI

'THE BASTILLE, THE BASTILLE!'

THE level landscape through which that rider flashed as a meteor was unspeakably solitary. So deserted the high road, that a stranger might have imagined himself in a plague-stricken or war-devastated region. Far afield were peasants turning hay or cutting corn, herds grazing here and there—that was all. The burning noonday sun shone upon a silent, inanimate world—a world that seemed given over to despair.

By château with weathercock and pigeon-house, pillory and carcanet, hated symbols of feudal sway, dashed the messenger, only his horse's hoofs breaking the lurid summer stillness—past church and presbytery, these too emblematic of privilege and extortion rather than of justice and brotherly love—past wayside Calvary, before which had lately filed

Protestant galley-slaves, for the moment Romanised, image-worshippers, doing homage to the first, last martyr of all humanity—past clustered cabins, windowless, one-storeyed, falling to ruin—past cornfield and meadow, grange and wine-press, their very abundance but an added terror to the peasant, and so much aggravation of his poverty, he galloped. Sentinel and watchman fell back, gates were thrown wide, bridges became clear. Every obstacle gave way before the herald of retribution, the forerunner of doom; on he flew, as that rider of Apocalyptic vision to whom was accorded a crown, who went forth conquering and to conquer.

The husbandman, sullenly measuring his tithes in kind for seigneur and curé, wheat and oats, hay and clover, the housewife, even more morosely counting her poultry, sure that the fattest must go as quit-rent, glanced up for a moment, then returned to their ungrateful task. What had horseman and his errand to do with them? Their lot was to toil and moil; for others the joyous season, the rapture of sowing and gathering in. Thus fared fathers and forefathers, thus would fare children and children's children. Little dreamed these toilers that every moment was eventful, pregnant of revolution, to be burnt into history with characters of fire.

As the afternoon wore on, the wide landscape was bathed in sultry haze; hot copperish clouds rested above the horizon, only overhead deep blue heavens showing through golden veil.

The heavy slumbrous stillness matched the torpid landscape; no smiling, alert figures abroad, only that of Labour, sad-faced, hopeless, pitiable to behold.

But the storm, the awakening was near. As the leaden, oppressive silence of nature precedes gathering tempest, flash upon flash, appalling thunder, deluging torrents, so was the passivity of the moral world portentous of change. All had heard the rider's words flung from him in his mad course as sparks from his horse's feet, none guessed that ere the morrow each would prove a firebrand, a sword for those to use who would!

'The Bastille, the Bastille?' quoth Fortuné. 'Sure enough that is the great prison in Paris. Yonder horseman, doubtless, is after some one who has offended the king. Well, what is that to us? Hand me back my money, Mother Douce, and let us have our dessert.'

They were half-way through their apples when a carter overtook them. He too must have been passed by the stranger, and carters hear everything.

'We'll bid the fellow to a drink, and hear what news he has picked up on the road,' said Fortuné.

The carter, bound from Genlis to Auxonne, although very willing to accept hospitality, could offer nothing by way of payment. He was, indeed, more ignorant than themselves.

Scratching his head with the puzzledom of Sancho Panza, he replied—

'The Bastille, the Bastille? No such seigneur lives hereabouts. Perhaps there is a fire at Seurre.'

'Hang the rascal for an idiot!' cried Fortuné, with a look of disgust holding his wine bottle bottom upward—not a drop remained. 'Would a messenger be despatched from Paris because a fire had broken out in Burgundy? Next time we will take care to get more news for our money.'

The trio, being now well rested, went on cheerfully, the women protected from the blazing sun by white kerchiefs tied under the chin, Fortuné wearing a broad-brimmed felt hat, in hot weather replacing the red woollen cap of the peasant, so soon to become symbolical of liberty and equality before the law—alas! of lawlessness also. Umbrellas, copied from the Oriental, and not as yet made to shut, were luxuries of the rich.

Here and there, above the level landscape, rose some château walled and turreted, or church spire with clustering hamlets. In field or vineyard a few country folks were at work—women brown as gipsies, thin as their bare-ribbed horse or cow, in scant, tattered garments, toiling with the men. As the wayfarers shouted a greeting to the nearest, they would shade their eyes and look up, then, nodding drearily, resume sickle or pruning-hook. The high road seemed deserted. Neither grand nor beautiful, the scenery nevertheless impressed Douce and Fortuné, now for the first time so far from home, now for the first time gazing on vast horizons, and, to their simple imaginations, boundless vistas, wide sweeps of pasture with herds browsing at large, hayfields enormous by comparison with their own. If still in France, could they be still in Burgundy, the land of vine-covered hills, coppice woods and forest, close-shut valley and croft?

By and by a pedlar overtook them, and pedlars were not like carters, they had eyes and ears. Now they should certainly learn everything.

But the pedlar, bound with mercery from Dijon to Seurre, had heard no more than themselves.

'The Bastille, the Bastille?' he said, looking wise. 'Something has happened yonder,' as he spoke indicating the direction of Paris; then he added in a tone of affectionate importunity, 'Come now, father, treat your good lady and pretty daughter to a newfangle apiece. I've the genteelest things in my pack, from a sou or two upwards.'

Fortuné reddened with pleasure. No greater compliment could be paid the little wizen-faced bachelor than the title of head of a family. He must purchase something, should it cost his last meal.

'A pair of garters, now, for mother; sure I

am she has a handsome leg and an ankle turned for the dance,' continued the wary huckster. 'As to the young lady—well, don't blush, pretty one! I'm a poor man, but I know my place; we'll not talk of garters for you, but of a silk kerchief for your hair.'

Whilst the women's eyes sparkled over the display of Lyons ribbons, English pins and needles, cutlery from St. Etienne, the two men slyly took notes of each other.

'No peasant he,' mused the new-comer, 'but, that I can swear to, one of my own craft.'

'Sure enough,' quoth Fortuné, 'I have seen this fellow's face before, and where else should it be but on the galleys or in prison?'

Freemasonry is of more kinds than one, and will tacitly assert itself. The pedlar now drew from skilfully contrived under-pockets little rolls of paper, small, printed, flying sheets, such as his beholders had seen at Dijon. The newspaper, rare enough in fashionable cafés, was quite unknown in rural districts. Marseilles soap, Rouen cottons, Flavigny comfits, Parisian knick-knacks, now lost interest; all three were fascinated by the sight of these new strange wares, to all present so many Sibylline leaves, unintelligible as Egyptian hieroglyphics. Fortuné handled the mysterious pages wistfully.

'Ah, comrade,' he said, 'if you and I were only scholars—what say you?'

'Do you suppose that a man's headpiece depends upon such rubbish as this?' retorted the pedlar huffishly, and replacing his packets. 'I flatter myself mine is pretty well furnished without what goes by the name of book-learning. However, we shall soon see. Folks in Paris live no longer on meat and drink, but on newspapers, so, leastways, I am told. Every day a new one is started.'

Fortuné was dying to put a delicate question. At last he got out timidly, 'May any one sell newspapers who can? are they duty-free?'

'Am I speaking to a man born of woman or a thistle-eating ass?' asked the other in a tone of profound contempt. 'Duty-free, my man? is anything as yet duty-free in France? Haven't we to pay tax for a sight of the sky, for the right to put one foot before the other? But by the time harvest is over—so folks say—there won't be a customhouse nor an exciseman left in the country. The States General are going to turn everything upside down—the peasant is no longer to be taxed instead of the seigneur, but the seigneur instead of the peasant—which, to my poor understanding, ought to have been the case long ago.'

'Holy Virgin!' cried Douce; 'and will the like of us become fine ladies and gentlemen?'

The pedlar, with Fortuné, was a martyr of the *ancien régime*, St. Paul of a criminal code unequalled for ferocity among barbarous nations, and upheld to the last by the 'mild' Louis Seize. Not an inch of his body but bore marks of civil inquisition, scourgings, brandings, tortures. Born democrat and revolutionary, he yet formulated a modest programme enough.

'Fine ladies and gentlemen? No, good mother—no offence, I fancy you would make as good a maid of honour as I should king's chamberlain!—but a whole skin, the right to turn an honest penny. Hurrah for the Three Estates, if they ensure us all so much!'

At a bend of the road he took leave, nodding adieux gaily. They continued their march, talking of what they had seen and heard. Was it possible that Dijon lay but three or four leagues off? They seemed already at the other end of the world.

Through the hot, slumbrous landscape they followed the horseman's track, questioning any one who came in their way.

'The Bastille, the Bastille?' and a shake of the head formed the invariable answer. As evening wore on, the silence and sultriness grew intenser. Harvesters and haymakers were still afield, but moved wearily, automatically, without interchanging a word, hardly caring to raise their heads as the travellers passed by.

Twilight there was none. Glowing day merged imperceptibly into night hardly less glowing. No moon lighted up the deep blue heavens, only stars, but the silveriness and purity of the atmosphere rendered every object visible. Far off gleamed the Saône, a line of sharp, metallic blue, above showed the tower of St. Jean de Losne, both beyond reach that night. The three footsore travellers now made for the nearest village, seeking shelter in a thatched wayside café, the poorest place imaginable, but affording all that they needed, a bowl of hot cabbage soup, rye bread in abundance, and beds for each.

The one guest-chamber, bare as a barn, led

out of the kitchen, and in each corner stood a curtained bedstead. Behind the folds of one Douce and Finette sleepily said their prayers; the second was shared by an honest charcoal-burner and his little son; the third Fortuné occupied; and the fourth remained at the services of any late comer. No one disturbed the heavy sleepers. Throughout that short summer night—the peasant's day began soon after cock-crowing—all was calm.

With the morrow tranquil nights and days came to an end for awhile. Not one but a thousand couriers were carrying the great news throughout the country, throughout Europe! The dazed world rubbed its eyes and repeated incredulously, 'The Bastille has fallen — the Bastille, did you say?

CHAPTER XVII

THE COMEDY OF REVOLUTION

WHAT was the transport of the travellers as at early dawn they came suddenly in sight of the broad, bright river, the canal, mere rivulet by comparison, joining the semicircle? To the simple women that luminous band of shining blue waters, making a loop about the landscape, circled France itself, was as the fabled serpent embracing the ancient world. By the low green banks lay many a barge. On the opposite side rose the fairy-like outline of Losne, whilst before them rose the famous little city that had once held the Austrian at bay. In appearance warlike still, to-day gates and bridges were open, crowds were flocking into the town from all parts. As Douce and Finette passed the sombre old church, both smiled at the figure of St. John over the portico, in his arms the symbolic lamb. It seemed to them a herald of peace and security. The vast underground cellars or storehouses of the citizens indicated great wealth, and the travellers gazed wonderingly at the barrels and heaped-up goods below, at the deep tapering roofs above, and countless tiny dormers. Walled-in gardens here and there also recalled Dijon.

But not Dijon itself had ever presented such a scene of tumult and confusion as St. Jean de Losne to-day. All Burgundy seemed flocking to the little port on the Saône, quays and market-place, streets and bridges crowded, business completely at a standstill, church bells ringing, drums beating, arms flashing. Musketeers were now marched aimlessly in one direction, dragoons as aimlessly led at a gallop in another, the multitude surging first towards this point, next towards that. The townsfolk had evidently gone stark mad, and new-comers caught the infection; for a brief space reigned universal delirium. Exultation alternated with suspense, and as there is always a vein of comedy in human affairs, folks were constrained to laugh and weep by turns. A shout here, and men, women, and children rushed forward as if for dear life. The cry of itinerant knife-grinder set all the men waving their hats and crying, Vivat! the distant rumble of a donkey-cart threw every woman near into hysterics. The parish beadle, not in the least knowing what he was about, donned cocked hat, scarlet coat braided with gold lace, and, staff of office in hand, solemnly paraded the town, the country folks falling on their knees as before the bishop himself.

The mayor, as much out of his senses as the rest, sent post haste for barber-surgeon in order to be copiously bled, next for notary to make his will, finally for curé to administer the last sacraments. The great lady of the place, Dowager Countess of Losne, sallied forth in curl-papers, slippers, and dressing-gown, and insisted on kissing her tradespeople, husbands as well as wives, grooms as well as serving-maids.

The great gentleman of the place, the Marquis of Seurre, made a round of the hairdressers' shops, shaking hands with the apprentices, and, by way of inaugurating equality, challenged each to a duel.

One worthy citizen, a timber merchant of irreproachable character, and meek to a fault, placed himself in the pillory, and ordered passers-by to gibe, jeer, and fling missiles at the greatest miscreant alive—a wretch for whom the wheel was too good.

An exemplary wife and mother, mistress of a highly popular cabaret and eating-house, the Cheval Blanc, seized a burning hot spit, and crying, 'To the Bastille, my fellow-townswomen, to the Bastille!' made for the prison, belabouring every one she met on the way.

Whilst all those in positions of authority were torn by conflicting motives, whilst the worst news could hardly damp the ardour of some, nor the best allay the fears of many, most lookers-on were simply bewildered. With Fortuné and his companions, the majority wondered if indeed the world were coming to an end. In one sense it had ended, with a vengeance. They had just arrived, and were slowly moving with the crowd, when a distant roar of voices, and sudden unanimous halt, announced fresh tidings. The throng paused as one man to let a mounted messenger pass through their midst; but outside the compact phalanxes, stragglers were running in breathless haste, anxious to forestall his message at the Hotel de Ville.

Fortuné's ears were abnormally quick, his movements also. With a triumphant huzza he handed on the news, to all present weightier far than that they had heard before.

'The Governor and Intendant have fled!'

Then, forgetful of his charges, he contrived to wriggle eel-like through the crowd, and off he sped, heading the foremost. Why should he not win the race and the reward? he thought. If the bearer of such intelligence were not handsomely guerdoned, then St. Peter himself, if despatched on an errand from above, would be sent away empty-handed.

The Governor and Intendant of Burgundy had fled! It was no less the odiousness of the men than of their office, that now made harmless citizens gnash their teeth and clench their fists menacingly. The very titles were synonymous with cruelty, extortion, iron rule. A governor and his lieutenant under the *ancien régime* could no more be humane, much less just, than bashaws of a Turkish sultan. Royal favour, place, even existence, depended on their capacity for crushing the people, their ingenuity in wringing the last sou from the poor.

In the case of these two, traditional hatefulness had been amply justified. Whilst the peasant and his little ones starved, their oppressors had amassed wealth after the fashion of Roman proconsuls.

They were gone, however, none knew whither, by summary flight staving off the hour of retribution.

The first sullen outbreak of long pent-up animosity gave way to wild excitement, threats and curses to frantic demonstrations of joy, and as in such moments men do not pause to reflect, being swayed by the first impulse, whether for good or evil, heroism or buffoonery, so was it now. The buxom goodwife of a cheap restaurant was hailed enthusiastically as the Immortal Maid, a scullion's turnspit acclaimed reverently as the sacred Oriflamme. Awful news flies apace, and the tidings just heard raised popular feeling to fever pitch. All now made way for this jolly Joan of Arc, this modern Jeanne Hachette, destined, none could doubt, to undying fame. When brandishing her spit, she rushed forward, the press broke up: one follower made a raid upon a shoemaker's stall, seizing awl and nippers; another dashed into a mercer's shop and caught up an iron measuring rod; others, more daring and bloodthirsty, laid hands upon butcher's knife and blacksmith's hammer and tongs. By the time the motley crowd reached its destination, such an array of domestic arms was formidable enough, whilst the shrieks, yells, and groans of the crowd might well have intimidated the boldest.

One prison under the *ancien régime* resembled another. The walls of each could witness of torture and martyrdom, agonies long drawn out.

The faintest show of compassion, the least vestige of feeling, would have incapacitated ministers of the ferocious criminal code then in force.

But sentinels and jailers are flesh and blood, executioners and torturers are human—at least to themselves. Was it likely that a humble De Launay and his underlings should coolly await tearing to pieces?

When the buxom landlady of the Cheval Blanc drew up her forces before the prison gates, all was silent and deserted—not a gendarme for her followers to hustle away, not a porter to be parleyed with through the grating.

'To the front, yonder friend with your chopper! Away, men, with mallet and hammer. Are we women to free the poor wretches only punished for being without bread to eat?' cried the good woman, working herself into a frenzy. What with the heat of the day, unaccustomed exercise, and, it must be admitted, somewhat burdensome proportions, her own movements were hardly equal to the occasion.

'Your axe, neighbour — have a care!' Setting his teeth, wresting the tool from a meek-faced citizen standing by, Fortuné sprang to the front.

Never surely had he been entrusted with task so welcome! As he sweated over the blows, a volley of threats and curses accompanied each. The very wood and iron seemed victims on which to wreak vengeance. Nor did he want imitators. Soon the solid oak showed signs of yielding, it swayed beneath missiles, ineffectual severally, but together having the force of a battering-ram.

At length, amid a hurly-burly that was positively diabolical, bars snapped, bolts gave way, doors tottered on their hinges. In this little Burgundian town had fallen another Bastille!

'Forward, my men! forward, sweethearts!' cried Fortuné, beside himself with triumph. 'To the rescue of our brethren within, chained like wild beasts, eaten up with vermin, scarified with the cowhide.'

In he rushed, brandishing his axe, close on his heels the heated, breathless, yelling multitude, one and all as excited as himself. Small wonder that not a soul was to be seen.

'The cowards! we'll whip 'em soundly and let 'em go,' cried the leader, peering about for jailer and turnkey. From end to end the place remained silent as a tomb.

At length, at the extremity of one dark, damp corridor, something did certainly move. A dozen stout fellows prepared for the important capture. But instead of frightened minion rushed forth a pretty, tame, well-fed cat, in the stampede of an hour before forgotten by its mistress, the porter's daughter.

Execrations were now replaced by uproarious laughter, puss was caught up, stroked, fondled, then the search began afresh.

'Ho there!' Fortuné shouted at the top of

his voice; 'where are you, my brothers? Never fear, no matter your deeds—highway robbery, assassination, false coinage, even heresy itself—you are delivered. Instead of rack, gibbet, and wheel, a hearty welcome, wine and a bellyful, ay, and money too, await you! Give a sign, then!'

Still not a sound emerged from the blank walls on either side.

'Sure enough the poor wretches are gagged. Don't I know how prettily we are made to hold our tongues in these snug quarters!' muttered Fortuné between his teeth. 'But we'll soon see. Can any one find a tinder-box?'

Groping about in the semi-twilight, he stumbled upon a crouching figure.

'By the holy apostles! a woman, worn to a skeleton, in her shift, cold as death! Cheer up, sister, we'll bring some colour into your white cheeks—ay, cover those bare bones of yours. A way—clear a way, good folks! let every mother's son see how honest women are treated in the king's prison!'

Triumphantly shouldering his burden, the little man backed towards the light, cheering up the victim as he went, the throng retreating also. And once more execration gave way to laughter, tragedy to burlesque. No wretched prisoner was this — instead, a dressmaker's dummy, used by Mademoiselle Aline, the concierge's daughter, in making her own gowns. When was opportunity for merrymaking wasted on a French crowd? Finding the prison tenantless, cells empty, porter's lodge and turnkey's posts abandoned, the multitude gave itself up to carnival.

The manikin was born in triumphal procession through the town, and not till every cabaret had been patronised, till voices grew hoarse and heads ached, did even the mistress of the Cheval Blanc recover her senses.

When Fortuné recovered his own, he found the tables turned with a vengeance. Instead of a dozen prisoners being let out, one had been locked in, Douce and Finette distractedly seeking their protector till nightfall. Then, tearful and downcast, the terrified women betook themselves to their destination.

CHAPTER XVIII

RED, WHITE, AND BLUE!

WHILST Pernelle entered heart and soul into the daily event, Laurent grew more and more self-centred. All the dogged sternness of Huguenot ancestry now came out. He dared not accuse his cousin and patroness of spiriting Finette away, but the poor child was gone, and her flight could only be attributed to one cause, Pernelle's fatal benevolence, her ambitious views for himself, her stickling by family advancement. Gratitude had no longer any place in the young man's heart, admiration was turned to disapproval, the liking of years vanished in an hour.

He returned to work, Finette's gentle image ever before him, determined, come what might, to keep his troth. As yet not a word beyond commonplace greeting had passed between the pair since the painful explanation of weeks before. Pernelle held coldly, or perhaps indifferently aloof; Laurent behaved as usual, only with more studied respect and emphasised humility. And meanwhile the clock and Revolution moved apace. To the good Dijonnais it seemed as if their Fleming on the top of Nôtre Dame had caught the general fever, so alertly he raised his arm, so energetically he wielded his hammer.

On the evening that followed the great news from Paris, Laurent awaited his mistress in the pretty room, boudoir, bedchamber, and counting house combined, leading out of the shop. Houseroom was expensive at Dijon, and the Beautiful Mercer here received alike guests and customers, signed negotiations and paid wages.

To her penniless, outlawed kinsman the girl generously allowed a certain sum monthly for clothes and necessaries, Uncle Parfait contributing towards the expense of his apprenticeship. Laurent had now come for this dole, never before accepted with such reluctance. It was a night of intense sultriness, and although the sun had set, shutters were still closed to keep out the dazzling after-glow. In semi-twilight he stood by the window, gazing fixedly, but seeing nothing, the very impersonation of sullen resolve.

All at once the door flew open and Pernelle entered, behind her a tall figure he did not at first recognise. Throwing the shutters wide, greeting her protégé in the unconstrained tone of former days, she turned to the new-comer.

'Dear, dear uncle!' she cried in the clear, exquisitely sweet and penetrating voice that might well have done duty for loveliness. 'A kiss first and your great news afterwards.'

The armourer threw down his cloak and bag, took off his hat, deliberately wiped the dust of twenty-four hours' posting from his face, then, rapturously as lovers, uncle and niece rushed into each other's arms. Only Pernelle had ever reached the depths of this outwardly cold, rugged nature; only Nesmond made Pernelle smile as a girl smiles upon her lover. Intellectually the two were one.

'Here is Laurent, I see. Who else has a better right to share our confidence?' said the elder man, holding out his hand. 'Who has greater reason to welcome the badge of liberty?'

Laurent glanced imploringly at his cousin, and uttered a word of proud deprecation. Too much engrossed to heed either look or speech, Nesmond added—

'The Bastille has fallen, as you know. That is but the beginning, the end we shall not see yet. Meantime'—

He had spoken with both arms resting on his valise. Watching Pernelle's face, evidently anticipating her enthusiasm, he now slowly undid the straps, and, without disclosing the contents, drew forth a rosette of coloured ribbon, red, white, and blue in equal proportions. Bending forward, solemnly, even piously, he fastened it to the maiden's bodice, kissing the token when his task was over.

'Red and blue, the colours of Paris?' asked Pernelle; 'white, the emblem of royalty?'

'Say of tyranny,' broke in the armourer, much moved; 'but Paris has conquered, Paris has saved the liberties of the world! Henceforth her Tricolour is the flag of France! Wear it proudly, girl. Try to live very long—the greybeards can but sow the seeds, for your children's children to reap the harvest.'

Pernelle pressed her lips to the badge, but could not trust herself to speak.

'And you, Laurent,' added Parfait, holding out a second favour. 'Little did I dream, my poor lad, that I should ever see such a day—each man's conscience his own—the Huguenot, the Jew, ay, even the negro, equal in the eyes of the law! Let us for a moment set other creeds aside and adore the power of retribution!'

All three bowed their heads as if in prayer.

'Blessed symbol!' cried Nesmond in a low, deep voice. 'To be tarnished, trampled under foot without doubt, and perhaps by those whom thou hast delivered, but vanquished, never! Oh! flag of France, flag of liberty, may we prove worthy of thee, may we proudly proclaim thy mission to the world!'

'Amen!' murmured the others, Laurent dropping on one knee, Pernelle with rapt face and clasped hands.

A moment passed thus, then Parfait turned to his knapsack. All three welcomed a relief from too solemn mood.

'Patriotism first,' said the armourer, smiling grimly, 'business afterwards. I had an eye to both, niece, in posting hither (I must leave for Paris again to-morrow). Look here: if I have not put at least a thousand livres into your pocket, my name is other than Nesmond.'

He walked to the door, peered out, reclosed it carefully, then, opening his kit, displayed rolls of red, white, and blue ribbon.

'Now, Pernelle, you have the start of all the mercers in Dijon—ay, in Burgundy! Forego a few hours' sleep, bribe or coax the little girls and your apprentices, every one in the house, to do the same. By to-morrow morning you will have favours enough for all Dijon, and hucksters hereabouts to boot.'

Pernelle thanked him warmly, and promised to lose no time. Not only would public spirit but interest quicken her fingers, she said. The shrewd tradeswoman knew well what store her uncle set by practical qualities.

He watched her take out the balls of ribbon, chuckling with triumph.

'I should like to see your rivals over the way when you take down your shutters to-morrow morning. Three or four hundred crowns ahead of 'em all, as I live! And before I forget it, niece, I wrote to your people at

Lyons, ordering a gross of each ribbon—you will get goods and invoice by next post. Well, I must leave you to your cockade-making. Come, Laurent, cannot you help your betrothed and her maidens in the job—cut lengths, ticket off, pack, or do something to aid the ladies?'

Laurent stood dumbfounded. Pernelle awoke as from a reverie. Up to that moment personal affairs and embarrassments had seemed trivial, less than nothing, to both.

The girl generously defended her kinsman.

'I forgot that I had not told you,' she said, anxious to get over the unpleasant disclosure as quickly as possible. 'I acted with some precipitation. Anxious to serve Laurent, I lost sight of one possibility, that he might entertain other views for his own future, have placed his affections elsewhere. Thus indeed it is, and there is an end of the matter.'

The armourer's habitually stern face grew a shade sterner. Romance had no part in his ethical programme. Marriage, above all other relations of life, should be in accordance with the seemly, the befitting—boyish, girlish fancy subject to reason. Love, in the sentimental acceptation of the word, savoured to him of something worse than folly.

For a moment he eyed his nephew, too indignant for reproach; then, with keen glance fixed on the young man's pale, resolute face, he said—

'Is this the way you repay her who has been the providence of your family? The name of this unhappy girl, sirrah?—unhappy she must be in having anything to do with one so reckless, so ungrateful!'

The angry speaker looked from one to the other. Pernelle hoped by silence to ward off the storm, Laurent desperately rushed to meet its fury.

'Cast me off if you will, uncle. In wedding Finette, the foundling, I defy my kinsfolk, but not my conscience.'

Nesmond turned away as from a gibbering maniac. Neither aversion nor exactly displeasure were written on his face, rather the pity engendered of contempt.

'The poor fool has no father. He must just go downhill as fast as he pleases.'

'Is affection nothing? Is a man's word nothing?' Laurent asked bitterly. His Huguenot blood was stirred, opposition but rendered him more aggressive.

'And a respectable position in life, bread to eat, clothes to wear, not only for oneself, but for wife and children — are these nothing?' was the still bitterer retort. 'I should have thought your father's family had been already dragged down low enough by fanaticism of other kind'—

Pernelle touched her uncle's arm entreatingly. Laurent no longer sought to control himself.

'Insult me if you will, sir, but at least respect my religion.'

'Religion, forsooth! Will religion suffice for the body? And the body has to be first thought of, whatever priests and pastors may say. Will religion repay your cousin, establish you in life, maintain your family, enable you to hold up your head? Look realities in the face. Confess yourself a visionary, a dupe.'

'Dear uncle, remember how much he has suffered already,' Pernelle put in softly.

Beside himself with irritation, the armourer continued—

'Are you stone-blind? Do you not see that the reign of these self-deluded teachers is over? Give me that ribbon on your breast, symbol of more rational creeds and humaner doctrines. Hold fast to your dreams and vagaries. Let them console you as best they can.'

He moved forward, and with rough gesture would fain have wrenched off the favour, Laurent as roughly averted the action; on both sides there was a rise of hasty passion. Swift as lightning, Pernelle caught each offending hand.

'Oh,' she cried, 'shall this thrice happy day be desecrated by family quarrels? Uncle, I cannot find it in my heart to blame Laurent. For my sake, then, do you forgive him and wish him well.'

The pair, outwardly reconciled, inwardly full of bitterness and resentment, exchanged sullen greeting, then went away.

Pernelle betook herself to her task somewhat sadly. Must every noble emotion be thus degraded by pettiness and personalities?

CHAPTER XIX

PERNELLE'S VIGIL

ON Thursday evenings, in days of Revolution as now, a military band played at the entrance of the beautiful Dijon park, all the townsfolk flocking thither to hear the music and chat with neighbours. To-night Berthe and Barbe had enjoyed the treat, returning home under safe chaperonage as the Fleming struck nine. Pernelle, rigid disciplinarian in all things, ever insisted upon punctual return. Five minutes behind time meant forefeiture of next week's privilege.

'Children, children, come here! See what Uncle Parfait has brought you from Paris,' cried the elder sister when she heard their voices outside.

'Oh, Berthe,' whispered Barbe, 'our new fans, perhaps, or our silk reticules!'

The twins would drop hints in Nesmond's

presence of what they hoped to get on approaching name-day or New Year; the mere fact of having given godparents such an opportunity seeming an assurance of possession.

'Humph!' retorted Berthe contemptuously. 'I hope it is something more worth having than a trumpery fan or hand-bag. You forget all about the States General and Uncle Parfait being deputy. He would at least bring us a gold snuff-box!'

Pernelle, without rising from her table, the heap of ribbons lighted up by a lamp, beckoned the pair to approach.

'Look,' she said, holding out a tricolour rosette to each. 'This is now the ensign of France, our country. All who wear it must love her, serve her, as hitherto folks have served kings and queens.'

Berthe took up the favour with ill-concealed disappointment. Barbe, ready to cry of vexation, still acted her little part. Whilst her twin sister was turning and twisting the badge, half in the mind to throw it down, Barbe officiously appropriated her own, looking up as much as to say—What do I not deserve for my understanding—my patriotism?

Pernelle, too busy to notice their behaviour, now applied a stronger test.

'Those who wear the Tricolour are expected to prove worthy of it. How many hours' sleep will you both sacrifice to-night for the Patrie?'

Barbe eyed Berthe, Berthe eyed Barbe. Both were glum.

'Understand, children,' Pernelle went on, in a voice rather of persuasion than authority, 'you shall not be called so early in the morning. But these rolls of red, blue, and white ribbon must be made up into rosettes by the time we open our shutters.'

'Why must they?' asked Berthe, with a blank look.

'Why? because every one will want to buy.'

'And why should every one want to buy?'

Pernelle tossed her head impatiently. 'Have I not explained matters a dozen times? Do you not see with your own eyes, hear with your own ears, what is going on? We are living in days of Revolution?'

'Will the Revolution do us any good?' asked Barbe.

'Does France hold only two inhabitants, by

name Berthe and Barbe Nesmond?' Pernelle replied severely. 'But no more of this foolish talk. Will you help me or will you not? Mind, I leave you free to decide. Patriotic service should ever be voluntary.'

Berthe for the life of her could not help the fatal query—

'You will, of course, give us something, sister, just as you pay your workwomen for over-time?'

Before Pernelle could make contemptuous answer, Barbe self-applaudingly whipped out her housewife.

'Here I am, sister, ready to stitch my finger to the bone—no mercenariness in *me*.'

The veneer was too transparent. Both minxes were ordered to bed, and Pernelle went on with her cockade-making alone.

Hardly had the door closed than irritation gave way to ardour, exalted hopes and bright fancies replaced personal annoyance. No fingers in all Dijon, perhaps in all France, so skilful as those of the Beautiful Mercer! To-night they were apparently endowed with superhuman speed and dexterity. Holding her ribbons in one small expressive hand, in the other, needle and thread, rosette followed rosette into the basket at her feet, as from conjurer's table. All were fashioned after the same pattern, yet each possessed a grace of its own. Again and again Pernelle had been pressed into serving some Parisian house. The Beautiful Milliner of Dijon put many a city rival to shame in the matter of bows and shoulder knots. Madame de Sévigné describes a certain marquis whose graceful salutation of partner at the dance was absolutely unapproachable. No one knew how it was done, but he made his obeisance so superlatively as to be thereby immortalised in her pages. Let none sneer at such immortality— better that renown than many a bloodstained aureole!

Pernelle's manipulation of ribbon deserved a similar honour. The yards of blue, red, and white took shape and elegance without any sign of effort on her part, proved subservient to her will as clay in the potter's hand. She had indeed no time for criticising her own work. The hammer-woman opposite struck the half-hours, her spouse still more sonorously sounded the hours, and faster and faster fell her rosettes, swifter and swifter moved thread and scissors.

not for a single instant did her energy flag, not for a moment was she conscious of bodily fatigue.

There is an inherent elasticity in French temperaments that often does duty for sheer personal strength, a power of resistance not to be computed of muscle or proportions. This slender girl, accustomed from childhood upwards to activity both of mind and body, accustomed moreover to forgetfulness of self, was a type. Here showed the bourgeoise at her best, no faculty wasted, no natural gift infructuose from disuse.

How, indeed, whilst thus occupied, could she dwell on personal affairs? To the ardent young patriot such a task was sacred, its fulfilment high privilege.

Snapping off thread with her beautiful teeth as milliners will, automatically clipping lengths of ribbon, giving that last adorable touch of finger and thumb to each token, she followed in fancy the mission of these baubles—no more to the eye, but endowed with talismanic charm, each a sign and a seal of brotherhood, alike symbol and guarantee of new conditions and ideals,

Pernelle had travelled more than most Frenchwomen, had visited Lyons and St. Etienne for the purchase of silks and ribbons, Le Puy and Alençon for the selection of lace, even Marseilles in order to buy West Indian gauzes. She had realised the poverty and degradation of the peasant; the iniquity of a triple law, royal, seigneurial, provincial; the hideousness of the criminal code; the dire effects of the Revocation.

Fresh in memory were the sufferings of her mother's family, beggared, outlawed, tortured, put to horrible deaths on account of their religion; fresh too in her memory the periodic famines effected by royal ordinance, men, women, and babes dying of hunger whilst the Bourbon despot held orgy in his seraglio!

And, young as she was, she could remember the sight of the king's galley-slaves passing through Dijon, chained in pairs, lacerated with stripes, their tattered garments swarming with vermin, worn to skeletons by hunger and barbarous treatment. And their crimes? This poor wretch had defrauded the king of a pound of salt, that had harboured a Huguenot; here was deserter from an army paid with blows, nakedness, and want, there an aged Protestant minister, his only offence being love of the Bible.

But Pernelle recalled more recent horrors. Not many years before, a smuggler had been publicly broken on the wheel at Dijon, none permitted to deal the final blow and put an end to eighteen hours' agony.

Oh, she mused amid her tricolour surroundings, the French people have suffered, Heaven knows how much! May they prove pitiful in their hour of triumph ; may their vengeance be justice and mercy !

Following this line of thought, she forecast the morrow, anticipated the future. She saw the nation rousing itself as at a trumpet-blast ; the oppressor brought face to face with his victim ; the weak venturing to confront the strong; from end to end of the land, a mighty rising up and levelling down. Then she beheld with the mind's eye, as in a vision, an august figure, new and strange to all beholders, for the first time and universally, worshipped, no other power contending her sway.

Had Justice or Retribution become the arbitrator, the destiny of France ? She paused aghast at the last image called up, trying to forget her uncle's words. But the mere recollection for a moment spoiled, even stayed her task. What if these badges, so glowingly fashioned, so hopefully breathed over, should engender feuds rather than brotherhood, enmity instead of peace? What if her own fingers should sow the seeds of deadly hate and implacable reprisals?

The Fleming struck midnight; one large basket was brimful of favours, and still yards upon yards of ribbon remained.

Pernelle was about to begin again, when she heard a soft tap on the shutter outside.

'Don't be startled, niece,' said the armourer. 'I knew I should find you at work, but now put by and come with me.'

She hastened to let him in, her first impulse being of alarm. Something unexpected had surely happened in Paris? Perhaps all was at an end, the Revolution throttled in its birth-throes, only direr and yet direr tyranny in store?

The sight of her uncle's face put an end to misgiving. A look of positive exhilaration lit up the usually stern features, contrasted as sunset gleam on granite crag, smile and rugged outline.

'Throw a scarf about your head,' added the intruder, giving no time for questions, 'and something about your shoulders. It may be cool up yonder.'

So saying, he pointed to the Ducal Tower, now standing out like a monolith of bronze against the clear, silvery heavens.

CHAPTER XX

THE BEACON FIRES

PERNELLE wonderingly followed her conductor as he made the best of his way to the Palace, ancient residence of sovereign dukes, for three hundred years seat of the Burgundian Parliament and States General; since yesterday become national property, one citadel more crowned with the Tricolour! Sultry as had been the day, a breeze now freshened the air. Nesmond raised his coat collar, and Pernelle tightened her shawl.

'It will be cooler still when we reach the top,' laughed Nesmond—he seemed in strangest humour; she never remembered him so garrulous, so expansive—'and I suppose you are asking yourself how we are to get inside the Palace at all? This is the Open Sesame, the universal key throughout France nowadays.'

As he spoke he pointed to his deputy's badge, adding grimly—

'And *lettre de cachet* also! If we open prison doors to the innocent, we must close them upon the guilty. But have a care, my girl!'

Through the narrow, ill-lighted, ill-paved streets, it was not easy to pick safe or cleanly way. The opulent, dazzling capital could boast of few conveniences for belated loungers. Here some housewife had discharged her dust-bin, there another had emptied her scourings; now the unwary stumbled upon curled-up beggar, now he ran against half-drowsy watchman.

A few minutes brought the pair to the Palace gates, hitherto guarded so royally by hussar and halberdier, to-day sentinelled only by a couple of gendarmes.

Few folks were abroad. The side-streets were solitary, but in the Place d'Armes a group had collected, all talking in low, eager tones.

Pernelle found herself among friends. The first to greet her was a worthy gingerbread merchant, whose bakery equalled in size and fame the celebrated ducal kitchen; next came up a fabricator of the unrivalled local liqueur made from black currants; a third owned large mustard-beds in the Plat de Langres; a fourth carried on the ever-prosperous business of pill-making, from time immemorial Dijon boasting of its superiority in this article of commerce. When pills are appetising, folks will take them whether ailing or no, and whilst other industries flagged, bolus-making throve like a young bay tree.

The four men, since yesterday become important civic authorities, with one or two others, now followed Nesmond and his companion inside. As doors flew open and officials fell back, the armourer could not resist a smile. To have put his thoughts into words would savour of arrogance amid these liveries and insignia of a vanished autocracy, a *régime* fallen with the Bastille. He only whispered in his niece's ear—

'When the fox smells a trap, the cocks may crow.'

He alluded to Governor and Intendant, a few days before enthroned with Oriental sway, now fled for their lives. The Burgundian Parliament had voluntarily surrendered its authority. Dijon, foremost of French towns, joined hands with Revolution.

One by one, and in silence, the little party climbed the stone staircase, a servant, lantern in hand, leading the way.

The Ducal Tower, or Tower of the Terrace, so graceful without, when reached from within suggests pleasure rather than warfare, courtly loungers rather than military reconnaître.

Below lie dungeons of sinister legend; the airy platform above were more fitly dedicated to lay or romance.

On a clear summer day, nothing can be brighter, more ingratiating than the panorama. All Burgundy lies spread at the gazer's feet, no land of surprise, but of grace and geniality, a land inspiring confidence in its inhabitants.

To-night, alike the dazzling tints of vineyard and pasture were obscured; invisible too the lovely blossom of the buckwheat, fields of flower the hue of sea foam amid the green and the gold. Featureless the Golden Hills, lately flecked with rich purple and crimson shadow; one vast monotone the eastern plain, by day a chequered scene of glorious colour. What colour, indeed, is not glorious under the warm Burgundian heaven?

If outline and detail were lost, night enhanced

the sense of space. As the beholders looked down from their lofty vantage-ground, they seemed to survey not only a province, but France itself; measureless as starry cope overhead, the dusk, beacon-lit world below. And as star followed star, every moment a new cresset appearing in the steely blue sky, so the vast gloom beneath showed gradually kindling fires. No sooner was a blaze discerned in one direction than corresponding flames shot up in another, by degrees the scene being illuminated from east to west. Grand yet awful was the spectacle, all the grander, the more awful because of its significance.

Whilst her companions, leaning over the parapet, talked to each other in undertones, Pernelle gazed silently, not at first realising the truth. On a sudden she caught Nesmond's arm.

'Uncle,' she cried in a tone of consternation, 'these are no beacon-fires, but incendiaries. Yonder burns the château of Luz; that of Til-Chatel too blazes. The towns aflame farther off must be on the Saône. I see the gleam of the river, and nearer, almost underneath, it seems'—

She stopped short, speechless with horror. The armourer turned from his companions, and answered coolly—

'On the outskirts of the forest? That is the château of Velours. Humph! much good will the poor fools get for their pains!'

The others tittered.

'A kinder-natured fellow than the Marquis de Velours never lived,' said the great baker; 'but he is a marquis, worse luck for him!'

'The Count de Luz is no villain either,' put in the distiller; 'only a count—as he will now find to his cost.'.

'And as to the seigneur of Til-Chatel,' quoth the mustard manufacturer, 'he will hang for his ancestors; that is quite certain.'

The fourth added in the same tone, not wholly of indifference, yet without a trace of horror—

'Yonder great lord on the Saône, whose towers make such a conflagration, his crimes too are hundreds of years old. Let him beware of the usurers!'

Pernelle could hardly believe her ears. Each speaker was an old acquaintance. She knew the inoffensive character of these men, their uprightness in business, their excellent domestic qualities, their benignity to the poor. Yet they could calmly behold such a scene as this—a province given up to fire, pillage, and perhaps massacre?

'Oh, uncle! oh, sirs!' she cried, almost beside herself with emotion; 'you are all now in authority, the fate alike of rich and poor is in your hands. Let the tocsin be heard, the soldiers called out, these ruthless deeds be put down by iron hand, or where will vengeance end?'

The four citizens glanced at each other, then at the armourer. Leaning over the parapet, looking down from his giddy eminence, Nesmond gazed around, counting and identifying the châteaux on fire. At last he moved away.

'Vengeance?' he repeated sternly. 'Do you imagine, my girl, that I have less compassion than yourself for the poor delicately-nurtured creatures rendered homeless to-night? Think you that I would instigate or condone brigandage, savagery? But beware how you use the word vengeance; call to mind another that was on my lips just now. Who devastated this very Burgundy, all France, with fire and sword in days gone by? Who induced plague and famine, wretchedness and crime, think you? The ancestors of our poor peasants now drunk with liberty—the forerunners of the crushed, trodden-down people? Does the guilt of centuries, the misery of millions, rest on the heads of shepherd and husbandman, artisan and labourer?'

He paused for a moment, then added, in still sterner voice—

'Is it thirst of spoil and bloodshed that has set yonder châteaux blazing? No; a hundred times no. What these incendiaries have set fire to is a system, none so iniquitous ever chronicled in history. Let them burn, the title-deeds of feudal sway, guarantees of tyranny, pacts of despots playing into each other's hands. On the altars of fanaticism fire has burned long enough and to spare. The altar of retribution now claims its own in turn.'

'Our neighbour is right,' said the gingerbread manufacturer after awhile. Taciturn as his friend the armourer, when he did speak it was tellingly and of set purpose. One might have supposed each speech was a contract. 'There can be no truce between noble and peasant till those title-deeds are burnt—better could it be by the public executioner.'

Turning to Pernelle, he added with a smile—

'Unfortunately the age of miracles is past. Be sure, mademoiselle, that we should all prefer a Revolution quietly brought about by a few advocates in cap and gown, and provided with plenty of parchment, quills, and sealing-wax, to all the burnings and plunder in the world.'

The others smiled; only Pernelle remaining lost in pensive thought.

'After all,' he continued, '' 'tis but the turning of the tables. To one château fired now, a thousand peasants' huts have blazed in former days; to one noble lady driving post haste from her splendour to-night, a thousand mothers, wives, and daughters of poor men have been rendered naked, homeless, ill-treated, outraged. You are right, friend Nesmond; Revolution is but another name for Retribution.'

The distiller put in grimly—

'If the poor souls get at the count's wine, they will drink beyond their understandings, whatever their capacities may be. He owns the best Beaune in the country.'

'All very well to pull down pillory and gibbet

before château gates,' said the third. 'As far as I am concerned, they shall stand at Dijon.'

'Yes, yes,' added the fourth. 'Why so waste time, neighbours? Bad laws have brought the country low enough, licence will not raise it up.'

One by one they descended in silence, Nesmond accompanying his niece, the others hurrying off to barracks and gendarmerie.

'Good-night, and fare thee well, love,' said the armourer, embracing her tenderly. 'Expect great, and great, and still greater news from Paris.'

He had crossed the threshold when he turned back and thrust a packet into her hand.

'Keep these passports safely under lock and key. No one can tell what a day may bring forth. A serpent scotched is not a serpent killed.'

Pernelle stood irresolute; energy and bodily strength still remained for her work, but heart was gone. The very sight of the patriotic emblems now saddened her inexpressibly. With quick, instinctive movement, she covered basketful and ribbons; then, putting away the passports, hastened to bed, hardly to sleep. What fitful slumbers came were disturbed by dreams of vivid painfulness and mystery. Now the stern figure of her uncle frightened sleep; he was remonstrating, bitterly reproaching her, she knew not why. Next the pathetic image of Velours stood in the doorway, on his gracious unforgotten features written sorrowful reproach also. Last of all, Laurent passed by, his face no less changed, a look of stern purpose transforming him from the Laurent of old.

When she awoke the Fleming had struck six of the clock, and all the townsfolk were taking down their shutters. The sun had risen splendidly on another day of Revolution.

CHAPTER XXI

SERIO-COMIC

Douce and her charge contrived to reach their destination somehow, and next morning gazed wonderingly upon the Saône.

They had seen the crystal-clear Ouche, as if pleased with such company, running alongside the no less limpid canal, in both mirrored poplar-bordered banks. For the first time they now beheld a broad, beautiful river, surroundings serving to enlarge and embellish. This level landscape, so uniform in tone and feature, would otherwise have seemed mean and unsuggestive. No vineclad hills, no rich woods and close-shut valleys, here delighted the eye as around Dijon; instead, stretched cornfield and fallow, their mellow gold and brown setting off the sky-blue waves, making them brighter, lovelier by comparison.

To the two artless gazers, this wide, softly-flowing river seemed a miracle, a god. The aspect of ocean itself could hardly have impressed them more. The Saône flowing close to flat banks, blue waves meeting yellow fields, looked so peaceful and friendly, it compensated for the vineyards left behind. Here then was a river indeed, how different to the Ouche, mere streamlet amid sedgy banks!

A couple of fields off lay Finette's home, tiled farmhouse with walls of clay and rubble; adjoining, all walled in, thatched barn, stable and piggeries, storehouses and henhouses. This homestead was also a novelty, grange and dairy, kitchen and offices, appeared enormous to their untravelled eyes. For the moment they forgot the cruel alarms of yesterday.

'Where does the Saône begin and end?' said Douce, after a pause of ecstatic bewilderment and admiration. 'But perhaps it has neither beginning nor end, Finette, like a fish with tail in its mouth, goes round the world, keeps it together? for if, as folks say, the world *is* round, something must keep it together.'

Just then she was seized from behind, caught

in the arms of a figure grotesque as mountebank or zany, despite her screams, kissed again and again. Finette, not wanting in courage, cuffed the offender to the best of her powers; she was about to make use of a stout stick he had let fall, when the two were held off at arm's length and a reproachful voice uttered their names.

'Fortuné!' exclaimed both women in a breath.

It was now their turn to caress, kiss, weep with joy. They straightway fell upon the intruder so roughly handled just before, neither of them having a word at command, too much overcome for the utterance of a syllable. When Douce had wept her fill, she began to giggle like a schoolgirl.

'Oh, Fortuné, my little darling, never, as I live, did I set eyes on such a scarecrow. Were I on my dying bed, the last sacraments ready, I should shake my sides with laughing—I know I should.'

Finette caught or rather emulated her friend's mood. She was not confident enough to jest on her own account. Peals of merriment now echoed far and wide; but the merrier they grew, the longer became Fortuné's face. He evidently regarded such an outburst as ill-timed, even insulting.

'Poor ignorant wenches that you are, I suppose I must make allowances for you. But take warning, Madame Douce, and you, Mademoiselle Finette! Those who make fun of the Tricolour in public places, will be taught better manners to their cost. Red, white, and blue,' here he proudly pointed to his adornments—' Red, white, and blue, I say'—

The very names set his hearers off again. Holding their sides, tears streaming down their red cheeks, they laughed more indecorously than before.

'Must I fetch some goose-girl or herd-boy to shame you into your senses?' the little man went on, with rising choler. 'Why, a brainless idiot would see nothing to grin at in me. A babe just weaned might clutch my ribbons, certainly, but grown women, one a wife and a mother, the other out of her teens, a notable girl too—I blush for you! Just cease that fooling for five seconds, and look up!'

He reared himself to his full stature, barely five feet, and, stiff and square as a recruit at drill, invited scrutiny. The mirth-stricken women only stuffed their handkerchiefs into their mouths, behaving with still greater levity. In very truth Fortuné's appearance was ludicrous enough. Some kindly bourgeois had arrayed him in old Sunday garments, sky-blue coat a trifle faded, red waistcoat, breeches the colour of fresh walnut peel, white stockings. The travesty might have passed muster but for the tricolour ribbons, hanging tassel-wise from hat and girdle, sleeve and small-clothes. He was indeed icicled from head to foot with the national colours, a Merry Andrew in red, white, and blue.

'You poor, dear fools,' he went on grandly—their senselessness rendering him all the more dignified—'you little know what you are gibing at; but, as I said just now, wiser folks than yourselves will soon be taught better manners, to their cost.' He pointed defiantly to his knapsack lying on the ground. 'I would have you to understand, then, that the Bastille has not fallen for nothing. Insult me, you insult the nation, France itself, the Patrie. I am no longer a jail-bird, wanted by police and gendarme, but a free citizen as good as any other. My business is to sell yonder cockades, by order of the Mayor of St. Jean de Losne, and all who refuse to buy and wear them will be clapped into prison—hung on the gallows if I had my way. Well, good-day to you, and good luck to all as empty-pated, say I.'

Muttering invectives, he picked up stick and knapsack, then stalked away. He had got a few yards off, when, with sudden movement, he turned round, and without a word threw a heavy object at Finette's feet.

It was Huguette's stockingful that lay there, through the worn threads glittered golden treasure.

The two women jumped up, their jocularity gone in a moment, both sobered by the sight.

'Fortuné, dear little Fortuné!' they cried, fast as heels could fly trying to overtake the fugitive. The incensed little man was captured, brought back, mollified against his will. In another moment all three were on tenderest terms, everything forgotten and forgiven. Squatted on the ground, an arm round the waist of each, Fortuné fondled first one, then the other. As children who have quarrelled, they rubbed cheek against cheek, ready for any atonement.

'We didn't mean to make sport of you, darling, did we, Finette?' said Douce. 'And oh, Fortuné, the night of it we have had! Holy Virgin, how many prayers did I not say on your behalf!'

'Your night? ah! I believe it; and what must mine have been? Finette, child, put that stocking out of sight; or'—a tinge of shame rose to his thin cheeks as he got out the rest—'shall I keep it for you a little longer?'

The pair looked at each other; somewhat reluctantly Finette was about to return the treasure, when he interposed—

'No; your money has already tempted me as St. Anthony was tempted in the desert. Hide it up—that is right.'

He watched her pocket the dowry, with Douce too delicate-minded to make further examination just then. Intensely relieved, Fortuné went on—

'I don't know what you thought when you lost me in the crowd yesterday, but my mind was made up, more than made up. Now, friend Fortuné, I said to myself, as the prison doors closed upon me '—

'Prison?' cried Douce. 'Grand Dieu!'

'Grand Dieu, indeed!' quoth Fortuné testily. 'Would the world have been made in six years, much less in six days, hills, rivers, quadrupeds and all, if you women had been by asking questions? The Almighty knew what He was about when He waited till everything was finished before taking a rib out of Adam's side for the making of you. Well, then, as I was saying, when the prison doors closed upon me, said I to myself, Fortuné, my friend, put a good face on it. Your hour is come.'

'But the prison doors were forced in?' Finette ventured to say.

'Do you suppose there is not a locksmith out of Dijon? Just listen, linnet-head. Of course a man must die some time or another, and a smuggler cannot expect to die in his bed, if he owns one. Hang me up and have done with it, I have nothing to say to that; but the rack, mother Douce, the rack, little Finette '—

The pair shuddered. He went on speaking between his teeth, as if indeed caught in some horrible engine, tortured in every nerve and limb.

'Take a villain's life, be he highwayman, burglar, assassin, heretic; but why make him suffer a thousand deaths beforehand? You know—but what should two harmless, home-staying women know of executioners and their ways? Fortuné, to his cost, knows a good deal. You must understand, then, that when a man is condemned for stealing salt, death is deemed far too good for him. A few years back he was tortured before trial and after; now only once—once! oh, God in heaven, such is the king's mercy!'

Douce and Finette put a consoling hand in his own; they seemed to witness the horrors he had conjured up.

'Think of it, my darlings,' he said, whilst tears of thankfulness streamed down his cheeks. 'All night long I lay with eyes unclosed, wide awake as Jacquemart on the top of Nôtre Dame. Courage! I said to myself; you have borne the lash like a man, have had your flesh torn with hot pincers, your limbs almost wrenched from their sockets. Pile these agonies one upon another, the rack, the boot, the thumbscrew, can't be much worse. And there is one consolation, they can't torture two lives out of a poor wretch; dead, he is dead for once and for all. Not the judges and executioners of entire France can bring him to life again.'

'But you were not touched after all?' asked Finette tenderly.

'Is nothing real to some people but the morsel of bread or bacon they hold between their teeth?' exclaimed Fortuné. 'No, little Finette, the Holy Virgin be praised, here I am, a free man with a whole skin. That does not alter last night. If ever a miserable sinner was given over to the devil and his tormentors, it was I.'

'There will be worse plague for most of us in purgatory, I'm thinking, my poor Fortuné,' Douce said, smiling.

'The simple as well as the wise should only talk of what they understand,' was the answer. 'Now let me supply your kinsfolk with cockades and be off; I've lost too much time already.'

The very mention of the Tricolour set his companions tittering; Finette's stockingful added to their hilarity. No longer irate at such high spirits, the proud pedlar of the nation accompanied them indoors.

CHAPTER XXII

IDYLLIC

IT never once occurred to the warm-hearted, motherly Douce that she was acting unjustifiably in weaning Finette from Laurent. Marriage to this good woman meant pairing off for toil mutually shared, and the daily interests and concerns of a hard, yet not uncheerful life. Douce belonged neither to the poorer nor richer peasant class of Burgundy; her ideal was necessarily the same, material exigences standing first, domestic affections regarded as matters of course, sentiment relegated to the last place. The view of wedlock as first and foremost a contract, entered into for the practical ends of society, is an inheritance, direct transmission of Gallic ancestry, the *mariage de convenance*, survival of Gallic institutions. Love in the modern sense of the word is also of modern growth. Thus Douce but entertained the ordinary notion.

Although only twenty miles from home, Finette found herself in a wholly new world, even Laurent for the moment forgotten. Everything here was new, strange, and absorbing. Shy as children on their first visit, the pair followed Fortuné into the kitchen. It was what is called in France the hour of soup, when fast is broken by a steaming compound of milk and water flavoured with bacon and garlic. On the long deal table wooden bowls were spread for each, low forms and stools serving for seats. In one corner of the vast smoke-dried room stood the curtained bed of master and mistress; in another, equally screened off by heavy beige hangings, that accorded their guests. Edmond, having charge of horses and cattle, slept on a rough shakedown at the entrance of the stables.

As the trio entered, their hostess was dishing up the soup. White-haired, bent with years, having a complexion the hue of vellum, she yet showed more vivacity than her niece Douce, and also far more knowledge of the world. Cézette and her husband were, indeed,

for the time and the place, superior people.
The fact of their childlessness and semi-
adoption of Edmond rendered them of tremendous importance in Douce's eyes.

'So you are bound to the fair at St. Amour,
my little old man?' said the housewife, glancing at Fortuné; despite his august mission, the
ex-smuggler and convict halted respectfully on
the threshold.

'I ask your pardon, good mother. I am no
mountebank cutting capers for the diversion of
empty pates, but a messenger of the State, the
nation.'

He proudly brought out his passport, signed
by the Mayor of St. Jean de Losne.

'I can't read, perhaps you can't either.
There's the seal, anyhow. You have surely
heard the news?' he went on, almost breathlessly impatient and contemptuous. 'The
Bastille is pulled down. All the seigneurs'
rights are to be done away with, the king is
going to govern by law and justice, and every
man, woman, or child who refuses to wear a
tricolour cockade will be clapped into prison.'

The good wife very calmly made the round
of the table, filling each bowl with soup, placing

17

an extra one for the new-comer — no more hospitable people than the French peasantry, even in these cruel times!—then she said with evident interest—

'Wait till my husband comes in to finish your story.'

So saying, she pointed to the place assigned him. Two good meals in the space of a few hours seemed to Fortuné's heated fancy the natural consequence of Revolution. Smacking his lips, he made little ado of the savoury potion; indeed, a second would not have been refused.

'Hearken to this stranger,' Cézette said, as Ambert came in, an old man with cheery blue eyes and shrewd smile, but of few words.

'He says—he says—but I don't understand a word. Let him tell his own errand.'

Fortuné had hardly begun, speaking with the eloquence of conviction and a well-filled stomach, when Edmond entered. He was a tall, comely youth, shyness itself, not needing his uncle's injunction of silence. All now ladled away, Ambert pausing from time to time to look at the strange narrator.

It was a study for a painter, the patriarchal

figure now for the first time brought face to face with the new *régime*, trying to realise its import, to understand its bearings, not only on his own case, but that of all France, all the world. He evidently recognised the fact that, baubles as they were, so many pennyworths of ribbon tacked together, these tricolour tokens did mean something. Without a smile, not in the very least disposed to quiz or banter this odd-looking herald, he ate and listened, listened and ate by turns. His wife too showed the same willingness to be enlightened. Thirty-five years spent by this good man's side had taught her to reflect also.

'Believe me or not, you can do as you think fit,' Fortuné rattled on. 'But why afraid to swallow this, that, or the other? You all know it, the Bastille has fallen. Can any miracle astonish us now?'

'The neighbour is right,' Ambert put in. 'What say the townsfolk?'

'Humph!' laughed the oracle. 'Douce has surely told you what they did yesterday, which is more to the purpose. Truth to tell, nobody has time to open his lips, every one's nose is in a newspaper. Newspapers fall from the clouds nowadays like snowflakes in January. The diligence from Paris this morning contained little else.'

Ambert's cheeks reddened.

'No impertinence, friend, but mayhap you can read?'

'Not I,' was the jaunty answer—nothing could humiliate Fortuné now. 'For all that, I can tell you what the newspapers say. A citizen was reading one aloud in the market-place as I passed by. You have heard of England, the country over the water discovered by Columbus?—a queer place, yet far ahead of us in some things. There, it is the rich who pay taxes, and not the poor as in France.- There, every man may say, write, or print what he pleases. There, all the grand seigneurs with their pillories and gibbets were thrown into the sea hundreds of years ago, and if the king commits a single act of injustice, off goes his head!'

Douce and the young people tittered. Ambert thought for a moment, then said wistfully—

'Friend, shall you be passing this way again? if so, bring me one or two newspapers.'

Cézette was about to utter a remonstrance,

but checked herself. Her husband never laid out a sou in vain; he could not read himself, but would, of course, find a lettered neighbour.

Fortuné fumbled and fumbled, then, to his own satisfaction and his host's intense delight, produced a couple of crumpled flying sheets, two numbers of the *Gazette de Paris*.

'Keep them and welcome,' said the little man, rejecting the proffered coin. 'You won't find therein much more than I can tell you. The States General are mending matters as fast as they can, and town and country are not behind-hand. Twenty châteaux were fired in Burgundy last night '—

His listeners laid down their spoons and stared aghast.

'You dear, innocent, sucking babes!' again laughed the exponent of the Revolution; 'you don't suppose that honest folks like ourselves would hurt a seigneur or his dame; it is not them we want, but their title-deeds, their parchments enabling them to pillory, flog, imprison, hang the peasant, to say nothing of extracting dues in kind, rights of pigeon-house, rabbit-warren, mill, oven. But no more. To-day I am servant of St. Jean de Losne, of the nation.

To-morrow I am my own master. You will see what you will see! Well, Tricolour or prison, which is it to be with the present company?'

Ambert smiled. His good sense told him how far the other was in earnest. By way of repaying his generosity, however, and pleasing the women, he purchased a rosette for each—not to wear, he explained, but to keep in case of necessity.

When Fortuné had taken noisy leave, Cézette and Douce betook themselves to their hemp-heckling; Edmond invited his future bride—so he was taught to regard Finette—out of doors; the old man was left alone.

He still held the newspapers, glancing from the Sibylline leaves he could not decipher to the insignia hardly less mysterious, those triple-hued ribbons, meaningless until yesterday.

Sifting Fortuné's words, making every possible allowance for misconception and braggadocio, he arrived at one conclusion, of itself rendering all others possible.

Time had made an awful leap. With the fall of the Bastille, the march of centuries had been anticipated in a day.

Book-learning, commerce with the outer

world, the give and take of public life, were not needed for his enlightenment so far. Men are taught history by life as well as by books; that is to say, what is history indeed, the existence of humanity. This white-haired peasant, turning from democratic organ to democratic emblem, from newspaper to Tricolour, vaguely realised a great truth. Retribution may be stayed, its progress arrested; surely, if slowly, the doom of injustice is pronounced, the penalty of wrong-doing incurred.

Pondering deeply, now with significant smile, now with a shake of the head still more suggestive, he resumed his labours.

He was too far-seeing wholly to rejoice. The hour of congratulation would come later, for children of babes as yet unborn.

CHAPTER XXIII

IN QUIET PLACES

ALL this time, amid the hurtling of forces now met in conflict for the first time, amid the shock of crumbling institutions and of a *régime* swept away for ever, life in quiet places went on as usual. Maidens were wooed and wed, babes were held over the sacred font, grandsires reverently borne to their last rest. Here and there, too, amid the less trodden-down populations, young and old would foot it merrily at twilight, keeping time with their own voices, needing no other accompaniment in the round.

Famine-stricken, plague-stricken regions existed, serfdom still disgraced the ecclesiastical seigneurs of the Jura, from end to end of beautiful France the curse of feudalism was apparent. But in this farmhouse on the banks of the Saône, with many another, might be found a certain amount of well-being. Ambert and Cézette toiled from four o'clock in the morning till nightfall; only a minimum of profit remained after the exactions of triple taxation, royal, seigneurial, municipal. On every side, at every turn, they found themselves in the clutches of some abominable law, law also being a triple-headed monster under the *ancien régime*. Now they must obey the king's behest, enforced by dragoon and musketeer; now of provincial governor and seigneur, enforced by gendarme and process-server. Their bit of land, however, with farmstead, belonged to them, for their cattle they could hire rich pasture, at the end of each year another louis d'or or two had been hidden away with the rest.

And they enjoyed one immense, one crowning privilege. Childless, they were yet free to adopt an heir and bequeath their hardly-earned property. The seigneury of which it had once formed a part, and on which it yet, in a certain measure, depended, had long since forfeited the right of mainmorte, of the Dead Hand—none held in greater abhorrence by the peasant, none more instrumental in bringing about the so-called Jacquerie, or burning of feudal title-deeds.

'The lad Edmond is of our kin, a toward youth, not, I deem, likely to waste his substance or fall into bad courses,' Ambert had said some time before Finette's arrival; 'but a man is what his wife makes him. We must marry our nephew first, and make our wills afterwards.'

Cézette and Douce could not write to each other, even if there had been rural letter-carriers to transmit correspondence. They nevertheless contrived to hold intercourse by means of occasional messenger, their little plot being concerted through the medium of friends bound to St. Jean de Losne on business. The two women now talked of nothing else, and ere Douce's departure everything was settled. True, not a word on the subject had passed between Finette and Edmond. Their compliance was a foregone conclusion.

'Finette has neither kith nor kin, but what may serve Edmond better, a few gold pieces with which to buy a cow or two,' Douce had said apologetically; 'and as to her religion, she'll keep that to herself.'

'Kith and kin, I take it, are much like dessert,' replied Ambert: 'unless sweet and sound, we are best without. Religion—well, religion is another matter; but Huguenots are now to be let alone, so folks say, and why they were ever meddled with I never could understand. They always seemed to me harmless enough.'

'Children born of this marriage must be brought up in the true faith, of course?' Cézette added eagerly. She rarely took such an initiative, but here convictions were at stake. Douce looked at her host.

The old man paused, then replied very deliberately—

'Shall I tell you my notion, wife? A time has come when we shall all think less of what folks *believe* than of what they *do*. Law will concern itself not so much with the affairs of another world as of this.'

His listeners had not a word to say. Evidently recent events and those flying sheets from Paris had set Ambert thinking. And others also! Each village alehouse was now a scene of animated discussion. One more instructed than the rest would read the last newspaper aloud, all in turn questioning, propounding, elucidating as best they could. A day, an hour of Revolution, was as a key unlocking men's understandings, widening their sympathies.

'And high time too,' the patriarch went on. 'Did ever government want mending as this? I can number threescore years and ten—what would my position be now had I only paid my own share of taxes, the seigneur, the priest paying theirs? I should be almost rich. Again, I have lived honestly, I have never, through fault or misfortune, fallen into the clutches of the law—what if I had? Why should a poor man accused of crime be condemned unheard, put to the rack, flogged, pilloried; and a rich man, committing offences a thousand times worse, get off scot free, just because he can show so many quarters of nobility, and in consequence is tried by his friends, or bribes his judges? No, no, my good women, we are all flesh and blood, as I fear some will now discover to their cost.'

Douce took her leave, having schooled her son beforehand—he was to seize his first opportunity of speaking out.

The next evening, ever memorable Fourth of August, Finette was despatched to help her young master, so she regarded him, with a load of hay.

In this favoured land harvests occur several times during the year, crop succeeding crop from May till October. Most beautiful is the aftermath of such a season, especially by the river and at eventide. Serenely yet proudly, broad belt of blue parting two golden worlds, the Saône flows amid cleared corn-land and meadow, the vast level landscape and wide expanse of gently rippling water imparting a sense of inexpressible repose. No gradations of colour are here, no indistinct blendings of light and shadow; all is clear, defined, harmonious, azure heavens, intenser azure below, velvety green and gold around, the general brilliance subdued as evening wore on. Hardly a breath was stirring. Bright and lustrous as cornelian against the sky showed red and white beeves, here, if nowhere else in France, filled with plenty. As the sun sank behind a ridge of poplars, bars of solid gold seemed thrown across the lawny reaches of the river, whilst its crystal depths took a hue of mingled rose and amber.

Amid this gracious scene moved the youth

and maiden, homely figures enough, yet not without a certain dignity and charm.

Both were barefooted and bareheaded; the weather was sultry, and Edmond had thrown aside waistcoat and neckerchief, displaying well-proportioned throat and muscular arms, browned by such suns from his infancy; tall, straight, and manly, he needed no adjuncts of dress or fashion. A kindly, upright, simple nature declared itself in word and smile.

Finette, too, would have been spoiled by corset-maker or milliner. Blue serge petticoat and loose cotton vest, permitting free play of arm and shoulder, were exactly suited to her occupation. In the clear glow, the two figures stood out as from painter's canvas. Without them the landscape would have wanted pathos.

Edmond, planted on the cart, stacked the hay as Finette tossed it up. For the most part their task was performed in silence; only when the last little rick had been cleared did the young man summon courage to speak.

'Let us rest a bit before returning home,' he said; 'you are tired, I am sure?'

'What good would the day be if we did nothing to tire us?' Finette replied. She was thinking—After all, what do griefs and disappointments matter? We work them off as the hours go by, and it will be with Laurent as with myself.

Edmond laughed. Not a trace of Laurent's bitterness or cynicism in this untried nature; homely, even hard, as existence had been to him, he knew nothing of inner conflicts.

'You may well say that; and better to tire for ourselves than for other people. My uncle and aunt are richer than you thought, are they not?'

'Douce told me they had laid by a little,' was the absent reply. Finette's thoughts were still with her absent lover.

'I am their nearest relation,' he went on, 'and they wish me to take a wife.' With a shy, swift glance he added, 'They wish me to marry you.'

Finette hardly changed colour. She also had been lessoned, but rather by the monitions of conscience than of others. It was her duty to release Laurent from his bond; he must wed the rich, important, and accomplished Pernelle, become in his turn a leading citizen. Herself beseemed a homelier lot, toils afield, shelter of thatched roof, a peasant's name.

'And I wish it too,' pursued Edmond, mistaking her passiveness, imputing her silence to maidenly reserve. 'You please me. I should like to spend my life with you—the first girl of whom I can say as much.'

Finette turned round quickly, and met his honest, affectionate glance. His last words made apparent all the cruelty of her dilemma.

'I hope you are able to say the same of me, then we shall be made happy all round,' he said. 'My uncle is getting old, he wants to settle me at once. You are very brisk, not wasteful about food, pleasant when spoken to about your work: all this delights my aunt, and of course I have their wishes to consider.'

'I am a Huguenot,' broke in Finette, putting the lesser objection first.

The young man tossed his head scornfully. 'If any one reproaches you with that, the worse for them, that is all I have to say. Look you, Finette, we do not spend our days in church, but at home; how we behave ourselves here is much more to the point than what we say when we get there. To each man or woman his or her own Sunday, I say.'

'There is another thing,' Finette went on, speaking very sorrowfully and with great deliberation. 'When in the town, in Mademoiselle Nesmond's service, an apprentice, her relation, asked me to marry him—some day, I mean, for an apprentice cannot marry. We were betrothed.'

'And what of that?' laughed the wooer lightly. 'In the town, folks are always betrothing themselves. So long as you did not care for your swain, what then?'

'But I did care,' Finette continued, too sad, too resigned for tears. 'That is why I came here. His family wanted to better his position, a rich marriage was arranged for him; so, not wishing to stand in the way of his fortunes, I accepted service here.'

'You did well. Ah, these town apprentices, they are not to be trusted, not worth a second thought!'

Finette was about to protest, but checked herself. Laurent was less than a name here—let folks say what they would.

'And every little girl has her fancies; but

you are a woman now, you know whether you could live happily with me or no. Well, shall I tell my uncle and aunt, they may settle everything else when they please?'

He received her softly-uttered affirmative, calmly as it was given. The poetry of that little love-scene lay in Finette's sacrifice. She decided to wed this honest fellow, toil by his side, minister to him and his, belong wholly to them, and all for Laurent's sake!

They returned home, chatting of material prospects, their first day of courtship no less prosaic than the future of such lovers. Only Edmond's confidence betokened deeper feeling, and Finette's growing sympathy, a tenderness that might develop with years, perhaps a safer preparation for married life than romantic passion?

CHAPTER XXIV

SALE UNDER THE DEAD HAND

REVOLUTION now marched with giant strides, feudalism toppled as a tree under the woodman's axe; the newspaper and the Tricolour made the round of France, spreading a creed hitherto undreamed of, equality before the law and freedom of conscience for all.

It is, however, one thing to issue noble propaganda and enact decrees in accordance with abstract justice, another to procure their realisation. As was only natural, indeed inevitable, between centuries of despotism and the advent of liberty, now intervened a reign of violence and blind passion. The tremendous flash of Revolution, of truth, dazzled men's vision, even the sober-minded no longer seeing clear way. Was it wonderful that enthusiasts, dreamers, above all, victims of the former *régime*, should grow giddy? Thus it came about that, whilst in a single night feudal institutions were annulled at Versailles, country folks, some of these the quietest possible, continued to take the law into their own hands. On that never-to-be-forgotten Fourth of August —the one Fourth of August in history—had been dispatched a triple-headed monster, the Geryon of royal, seigneurial, ecclesiastical privilege. During the sultry hours of a harvest evening, *taille* and *corvée* followed *lettre de cachet* and judicial torture; confiscated with as little ceremony were the rights of excommunication, of holding slaves, of suppressing the written word and speech. The French nation went to bed in social, moral, and spiritual bondage, and woke up possessed of a Habeas Corpus Act, of trial by jury, of a free press and liberty of conscience. A people hitherto held in leading-strings had declared itself adult, proclaimed its own majority. Fact is more akin to the popular mind than theory, and especially those who had been galled by feudal tyrannies now showed lawless impatience. Fast as their legislators could abrogate and decree, their own initiative ran on before. Seigneurial rights had ceased to exist, yet châteaux were ransacked and title-deeds blazed. To the simple, unlettered peasant these parchments were so many warranties of subjection; his freedom, his very manhood, depended on their total disappearance.

Ready, of course, to egg on the reluctant and aid the more willing, were law-breakers by calling, ragamuffins and desperadoes ever alert for pillage, men to whom the Revolution meant licence only; the scum of town populations now betaking themselves with more hope of advantage into the country.

The morrow of this unique Fourth of August, to be blazoned in history with gold and purple characters, saw Huguette's former neighbours astir.

'You'll just go and have a look at Velours' vineyard?' Jeanne had said at soup-time to Pierre.

Democratic to the core, democratic without knowing it, country folks among themselves seldom used high-sounding titles. Marquis, Comte, and Monsieur had been alike dropped long before Citizen came into fashion.

'We may as well,' quoth Pierre. ''Twill go for a song.'

It was the long-suffering mothers of France who initiated the Revolution, the wives of the people who stormed the Bastille. Jeanne tossed her head scornfully. The Declaration of the Rights of Man now being formulated at Versailles was no revelation to merciless reasoner.

'Well worth while wasting tinder and tow on his château. Why, Velours' parchments are not worth a sou; his father, so folks say, had to sell silver plate and even madame's lace flounces for bare subsistence.'

'That may be,' said Pierre in his slow, sullen way. 'The present marquis may possess no more land than we two, but he is a marquis, which makes all the difference. As a marquis, not as a man, he is in bad case now. Think of it, woman : I snare a seigneur's rabbit or pigeon on my own field, and am sent to prison or the gibbet for it; he may let his rabbits and pigeons devour my crops to the last ear and blade. I may not sow corn till the seigneur's is in the ground, cannot get it to market till I have paid his tenths and his tolls, cannot so much as grind a sack of wheat where I please, bake a loaf in my own oven; and, to speak as a vintager, not a barrel of wine must I offer for sale till Monsieur le Comte has made a good price of his own. Let the accursed parchments burn, say I'—

'Folks declare that the law is going to do away with them,' interposed the wife, 'and high time too.'

'Then we will help the law,' Pierre replied.

'Look you,' Jeanne said. 'We see plain enough what is coming. The devil could not ride his high horse for ever. But leave others to their château-burning, don't you and Anatole get yourselves into trouble.'

Anatole was their first-born.

'When you see me brandishing a pitchfork in my night-shirt, it will be time to cry—Have a care,' was the answer. Whilst resolute to keep out of harm's way, Pierre was quite ready to profit by the aggression of others.

Once more Huguette's little domain became an animated scene, but how different the aspect of bystanders now! On that dewy, tranquil morning three months before, folks had stolen up by twos and threes, talking in undertones, eyes cast down, their demeanour becoming the precincts of death. Peaceful as the season, calm as the landscape, had then been alike voice and gesture, no vindictiveness disturbing young or old, long-suffering or impatient.

To-day all was changed. Noisily and ostentatiously, a look of assumption, even bravado, changing every sunbrowned, toil-worn face, the villagers hastened forward. Cabin, field, and vineyard were to fall under the auctioneer's hammer, escheat of the seigneur by virtue of mainmorte, the hated law of the Dead Hand. It was not so much the sale as the occasion that attracted people. These dark looks, these sinister whispers, seemed to say—

'Can such things be to-day? Three months ago the Bastille had not fallen, but now—?'

'Eh, Félix and good mother Douce, you've come for a bid, have you?' was Pierre's greeting as the meek-faced pair advanced, perhaps the only lookers-on who had come for no other purpose. 'And you, father Robert, and Victorine—Etienne too! Well, we shall have to scramble for it on hands and knees. And mind you'—.

Here he dropped his voice to a whisper, and added—

''Tis said that Velours is only just in time,

that when the law is altered, which it will be soon—the law of the Dead Hand, I mean—there will be no more properties of widows and childless folks for seigneurs to snap up.'

Douce put in very gently—

'Velours is not a hard man. I don't think any of us can say that of him.'

Pierre laughed gruffly.

'Little enough he has had to be hard with, good mother. But he is a marquis, worse luck for him in these days.'

'He gave away bread during the famine, as long as he had any to give, poor soul,' Douce again ventured to say.

'And his grandfather hanged mine for a trespasser on his game preserves,' was the savage reply. 'I tell you, my good woman, Velours has not been burnt out of house and home because he is a villain, but because all seigneurs have been made villainous by the law.'

Poor Douce felt overcome by these arguments.

'I don't like the look of Pierre, nor of Anatole, nor even of old Robert,' she whispered to her husband. 'I am convinced that they are not here to bid, but to make mischief. Let us steal away.'

Félix shrugged his shoulders without budging an inch.

Rural life under the *ancien régime* was monotonous as that of a prison; with many another, Félix welcomed anything in the way of gratuitous excitement. He determined to see out the auction.

The scene grew every moment more animated. Never before had such a sale attracted purchasers so numerous. A poor hovel and outhouses to match, an enclosed vineyard, cornfield and cabbage garden, the entire area being under two acres, these made up the lot. Folks peered hither and thither, one tapped the mud-built walls to test their soundness, another with his heel turned up the soil in order to judge of its quality, a third with outspread arms measured the cabbage garden, a fourth counted the vinestocks in a row. And meantime tongues moved glibly.

'Sure that is some fine bourgeoise yonder,' Jeanne said to Pierre in a grudging tone. 'One thing is certain—if the townsfolk want to buy, we stand no chance.'

Douce at the same time whispered to Félix—

'Don't let us go outside the vineyard. That lady just come up in a calêche is Finette's former mistress, the milliner opposite Nôtre Dame. I am not to tell her where the child is, and I won't—nothing shall make me!' reiterated the good woman, screening herself behind some broad-shouldered neighbour.

'There is another calêche, and another. I suppose the citizens want to build châlets up here,' Félix replied, with a crestfallen air. 'Worse luck for us! However, we'll wait and see.'

Drawn up in single file alongside Huguette's domain, the hooded carriages made sombre undulations above the bright picture, dazzling foliage of vine and young rye, creamy blossom of buckwheat ready for the sickle. As yet their inmates remained inside. Once ensconced, it was no easy task to descend, the pre-Revolutionary calêche needing as much reform as the pre-Revolutionary criminal code. One advantage must be named, that of displaying a lady's ankle as she descended, and of affording opportunity for graceful gymnastics.

From under the hoods peeped fashionably

frizzed and coifed heads of city madams, whilst standing by, chatting of the business in hand, the scenery, the last news from Paris, stood cavaliers, husbands, brothers, or men of business, come to represent them at the sale.

Each group now became the object of curious, almost aggressive, scrutiny on the part of the other. Peasant and bourgeois were not so widely separated as peasant and noble, but a tremendous gap lay between the two. The bourgeois was also a favoured class; on his head rested the crime of accepted prerogative. Even his presence here aroused resentment. Could not a few villagers haggle among themselves for a parcel of land? Must rich shopkeepers, forsooth, run up the price?

Even more unsympathetic were the intruders.

'How uncouth in appearance are these rustics!' quoth one.

'How boorish their behaviour!' added a second.

'Humph! we are evidently not needed here.' remarked a third.

'I don't wonder at châteaux being burned,' cried a fourth.

Only Pernelle held her peace. The contrast between her own condition and that of these brethren and sisters humiliated her. What had made them sordid, bitter, and malevolent? Who was responsible for their poverty and haggardness, their premature look of age and decrepitude?

CHAPTER XXV

'THE DEAD HAND'

'So, Mademoiselle Pernelle, you are going to buy a vineyard and build what they call over the water a cottage? Spend your Sundays out of town, eh?'

Pernelle smiled at the speaker, cloth merchant from her own street, and let him have his way. The gaping outside world must be satisfied with a motive of some kind, whenever we do an unusual thing. Suburban retreats from the torrid Dijon summer were not in her thoughts just then, nor were her quick business faculties alert. She had come to buy, that was all. The profitableness of such an investment was a secondary matter.

'Good day,' said another neighbour, portly hardwareman from the next street. 'We won't quarrel about this plot of ground, mademoiselle, but I have long wished for a summer-house and garden within a walk of the town. And,' here he dropped his voice, 'if we are both disappointed to-day, never mind. The seigneurs are taking fright, and no wonder. All Burgundy, all France, will be in the market before the year is out.'

He glanced approvingly from her tricolour rosette to his own. 'I mean to say that things are moving fast in the right direction. Why should one man possess half a province which he turns into a desert, whilst thousands of poor wretches cannot obtain as much as a square foot? All our people want is a bit of land, and see what they do with it when they get the chance.'

Beyond Huguette's tiny croft and plots of rye and cabbage, lay others cultivated with equal care, not an inch wasted.

The speaker continued in the same good-natured, half-contemptuous strain, much as if he were criticising an alien or inferior race—

'The peasant is a good Catholic—as Catholics go. Let the curés, however, say what they choose, Mother Earth is his goddess, the almanack his prayer-book, the seasons his patron saints. Paganism, you may call it—no other creed will save France. But who in the name of Heaven is yonder scarecrow?'

It was Fortuné, Renard the ubiquitous. No longer icicled with tricolour streamers, in his sky-blue bourgeois coat, faded red satin waistcoat, and breeches the hue of freshly peeled walnuts, he yet presented a nondescript appearance enough, his assumed importance heightening the effect. Had the withered little man alone and unaided stormed the Bastille, had he been named by the States General Governor of Burgundy, he could not have showed more assurance. Alternately crying his wares—the ex-smuggler to-day hawked newspapers—and shouting 'Long live the nation!' he made his way through the crowd. Old acquaintances and boon companions were nodded to, that was all. Condescension on his part did not go so far as a single—How d'ye do.

Neither auctioneer, valuer, notary, nor their clerks, had as yet arrived. Coolly taking up his position on the spot reserved for these important functionaries, springing to the improvised platform opposite the cabin door, he opened his harangue, none more genuine delivered during the Revolution.

'My little innocents and white-haired bantlings, poppets who have seen threescore years and ten, weanlings who limp upon crutches, you pretty kids, lambkins, puppies, and goslings, come into the world before myself. Oh! you open your eyes, do you, darlings, your ears too? as well you may. Hearken, then,' here he waved a newspaper above his head. 'The world has turned upside down since folks put on night-caps and bed-gowns two days ago—ay, and tumbled head over heels like Harlequin at the fair. You don't believe me? Here you have it, then, in black and white'—

One listener, more officious than the rest, would fain have snatched the newspaper from his hand. Fortuné deftly evaded the gesture.

'Oh! you want to show off your book-learning, monsieur, do you? but wait a bit, my fine scholar. If I can't make out these dots and twists and twirls and whirligigs, I can remember what wiser folks tell me, write *that* down in my own way, and on something more solid than paper.'

As he spoke, he tapped his forehead knowingly.

'Bravo, bravo!' shouted a bystander; 'out with your wonderful news, then,' his interruption being followed by a peal of laughter. The country folks all knew the odd little figure now so pompously haranguing them from the estrade. His appearance, presence, and self-assumption seemed an excellent joke. Fortuné was not to be laughed out of countenance or out of his place.

'What did I tell you on this very spot three months ago, when the vine was in flower and Huguette lay dead? You all giggled then as you are giggling to-day; but wait a bit, listen awhile, you will see who was right, you or I.'

Huguette's name now passed from mouth to mouth; one by one, his audience grew silent and attentive; the bourgeois lookers-on, farther off, also watched and listened. How diverting are these rustics! their faces said; how more than diverting will be yonder orator's discomfiture when auctioneer and notaries arrive!

Fortuné, small and spare as he was, possessed a voice of amazing volume and piercingness. Far and wide his utterances could be heard now. The crowd of villagers became mute as folks at a funeral, their neighbours from the town gradually forgot to titter. Every word reached the farthermost present.

'When the vine was in flower,' continued the speaker, 'we were all gathered here as we are gathered at this very moment. I repeated Huguette's dying words. Poor soul, she had no more book-learning than myself, but for all that she was a master-woman'—

He took off his hat, indicating respect for theme so solemn, several standing by did the same, then he went on in a grave and yet graver tone—

'" Horror and darkness are upon the land, but following after, days such as the like of us have never seen. Heaven has not forgotten the peasant. It is night with him now, the dawn is there!"'

Imitating the dead woman's tone and action, he repeated the words, as he did so, pointing eastward. Then, with a sudden brusque movement, look, tone, attitude changed from funereal sobriety to exuberant mirth, he tossed his hat in the air, footed a measure, blew kisses to Douce and Jeanne, finally resumed his discourse.

'Those who can may read for themselves;

meantime, here are the chief items of news, news enough to raise the dead from their graves.'

He held up his flying sheet, and, finger on paragraph, began to read, rather to repeat, his well-conned lesson. Memory does not necessarily imply book-learning, and indeed often the reverse, some of the emptiest pates in the world being steeped through and through with printer's ink.

'Hear, then, what took place at Versailles on the Fourth of August, in the year of grace seventeen hundred and eighty-nine. Item one—This does not concern a vagabond like myself, whose taxes'—here he rubbed his back, arms, and legs—'have been taken out with the cowhide in kind; but what say you, friend Pierre, to this decree of the National Assembly, and you, Father Robert? From to-day, dukes and marquises, ay, bishops and curés, are to pay king's taxes as well as you two and other poor clodhoppers like you!'

'Let some one read the Paris journal to us all,' cried an impatient hearer.

Fortuné negatived the proposal with a huffish air, and pretended to pocket his newspaper.

'Will every one be quiet?' he asked. 'I tell you I know what is printed here as well as those who spoke, penned, and printed it. Item two, since you let me proceed: Seigneurs abolished; that is to say, from the said Fourth of August, the seigneur who was a god is done away with. No more scouring across the peasant's cornfield with horse and hounds, no more pillories and gibbets at his château gates, no more pouncing upon the poor for tenths and twentieths, no more dovecots and rabbit warrens, and—open your ears, Jeanne, Douce, and all good women—no more carrying your corn to the seigneur's mill, nor dough to the seigneur's oven.'

There was such conviction in Fortuné's voice and manner, such a defiance of doubt in his conduct, that loud vivats now rent the air. The reformations so passionately desired, so hoped for against hope, were believed in, and on the strength of an outlaw's word. With a lie on his lips, would he have ventured to stand there, not only all the neighbours but townsfolk being by, and not only neighbours and townsfolk, but a stray gendarme or two, a process-server, even an officer of the excise?

Louder and louder grew the huzzas, louder and louder Fortuné's voice.

'Will you let me proceed, neighbours?' he cried once more. 'The best is yet to come. Well, we are getting on. Item—is it three, thirteen, or thirty?—you will find it here, those of you who can read. Yesterday, then, the law was a commodity to be bought, justice a matter of louis d'or (easy to understand how little we have ever got of it—eh, neighbours?). To-day, yes, to-day, the new order of things begins. No more— And that reminds me'—

Just then three officious personages were seen elbowing their way towards the estrade. The new-comers, who had the moment before alighted from a calêche, carried large shiny black portfolios, and the foremost wore notary's cap and gown. Bustling forward, evidently much surprised at not being made way for, they caught the words—' That reminds me of mainmorte, the law of the Dead Hand, according to which Huguette's vineyard was to be sold to-day. Don't you know it, gentlemen,' he added, speaking to the new-comers, 'and you come from Dijon? you will do no business here to-day. Not my effrontery but the newspaper tells you that. Read if you will.'

So saying, he tossed a journal to the foremost of the three. Dashing it contemptuously to the ground, urging on his companions, the outraged auctioneer made for the stand. A moment later, the hitherto gay and peaceful scene became one of violence and confusion. Cheers and vivats gave way to hisses and execrations, fisticuffs were freely exchanged, the representatives of yesterday's law were driven back, hustled, buffeted. In the horrid mêlée that ensued, there were soon numbers set against three.

CHAPTER XXVI

LOVE AND REVOLUTION

A FEW minutes before, Pernelle had received unexpected greeting. Whilst watching the peasant folk and listening to their tribune, a man's figure passed and repassed her calêche, then, having evidently summoned courage to approach, the stranger addressed her by name. It was some one she knew, yet at first sight failed to recognise. Tailor and barber had transformed the out-at-elbows seigneur into a meanly-clad but respectable gentleman. To-day the Marquis de Velours wore neither tattered lace, faded brocade, nor silver shoe-buckles engraved with the *fleur de lis*; instead, the sober middle-class costume borrowed from America and England. Black cotton stockings, long-lappeted coat and breeches of dark cloth, made him less picturesque, they did not detract from a certain air of decayed gentility and forlorn high breeding. It was curious that, although so lately in her thoughts, although she was here on his account, his presence should come as a great surprise.

And Pernelle Nesmond, no fine lady accustomed to conceal her thoughts, but a woman of business, direct, outspoken, straightforwardness itself, at once let him see what was in her mind. None stood by, the hood of the calèche lent security from eavesdroppers. With a glow of shame, not for herself but for him, and a tone of keenest reproach, she exclaimed—

'You are going to desert your country in its hour of need—to emigrate? Your dress tells me that.'

He confronted her discommending look with a sad smile. Bareheaded—before a lady of royal house he could not have shown more deference—he said—

'My country is synonymous with my king. You forget, mademoiselle, that I was born before yourself, too early for Revolution.'

A noble-minded, enthusiastic woman, especially if conscious of youth and beauty, ever clings to the hope of winning others, making converts zealous as herself.

'But not too early for redress,' she said, speaking very quickly, feeling that this might be her last chance—she must make an impression now, or perhaps would have no other opportunity. 'Not too early for example, and the example of one in your position may do so much. What France needs now is initiative, self-sacrifice in high places. Unless the necessity of Revolution is acknowledged, acted upon, alas for us all!'

He was in no hurry to finish the argument, although sure of being worsted. Leaning forward, his arms resting on the door of the carriage, he replied, again smiling—ever with the smile of a desperate man—

'The necessity you speak of seems already to have been acted upon with a vengeance. That is to say, if all we hear is true. But, mademoiselle, were my pitiful example indeed worth anything at all, just pause, reflect—is it likely that I should throw over inherited creeds, traditions, ideals, in an hour and at the bidding of a mob?'

'Creeds, traditions, ideals, may be falsified, proved untenable, even iniquitous,' Pernelle put in.

'Granting that—granting more than that, is my dilemma less cruel? I should rather say, is the path of duty thereby obscured, rendered doubtful? Great causes also become personal, are not to be separated from their leaders. Am I, from your point of view, traitor to the people? Should I not prove doubly, trebly a traitor, by casting in my lot with theirs?'

'Oh,' Pernelle cried, her voice heavy with suppressed misgiving, 'must it come to that—a severance of the French people into two camps, warfare of brethren?'

He was silent for a moment, his expression became grave as her own. Then the reckless gaiety of his nature asserted itself. The country verged towards an avalanche, none could predict the morrow; whatever might happen, his own case was past remedy.

But the sun shone over the pleasant scene, a small hand imploringly touched his own, a sweet, passionate voice recalled the fact of being appealed to, confided in; bent towards him was the one face he deemed adorable.

'Why so cast down?' he said. 'The greatest misfortunes often prove sovereign cure. Who knows what a universal deluge may not do for us from a moral point of view in evolving the heroic? Even a poor creature like myself may vindicate himself; and let me tell you'—

Here he dropped his voice, and—was she dreaming—did a tear dim his eye?

'Let me tell you for once and for all, had I not a touch, a vestige, of the heroic in me, you would need say no more. For the sake of a word, a smile, I were on your side, won over to the popular cause, the hated Tricolour—traditions, creeds, all the fine things I boasted of just now cast to the four winds.'

A few months before, the young milliner would have resented such a speech as an affront, no honest gentleman, indeed, would have ventured to make it. The fall of the Bastille and the Fourth of August had destroyed feudalism; the admission of the Third Estate, of the Commons, to the deliberations of the assembly with noblesse and clergy, had broken down social barriers. A few months before, the marquis could not have spoken, Pernelle could not have listened. Unconsciously, in spite of himself, he was influenced by the Revolution.

'Say that you believe me,' he added; 'my poor little bit of heroism, my unworthy sacrifice, will then have had their reward.'

'Why should I not believe you?' Pernelle said, simply and very sorrowfully. She also was influenced by the social aspects of the great movement. The declaration of a noble marquis to a tradeswoman called forth no blush of shame, no haughty rebuke. It flashed upon her as a revelation that this idler amid dilapidated surroundings, this social nonentity despised by her own class, had yet something in common with its leaders. His present aloofness from people and bourgeoisie might be due to magnanimous scruple. And, least sentimental of womankind, schooled to regard love in the romantic sense as unbecoming, even immoral, Pernelle was yet capable of deep feeling. Velours' shattered fortunes had already touched her, his loneliness touched her now, no less so his craving for sympathy and affection. But his next speech was to bring them still nearer together.

'There is a bond between us,' he added, the pitifulness of his story emboldening him, her tear of fellowship making the rest easy. 'Our good friend, Father Albin—whose guest, I should rather say, whose dependent I am—has, I see, blabbed. I know you, high-minded benefactress even of your enemies'—

'No, no, do not use that word of a fellow-countryman,' she interposed passionately.

'But it is the true one, no other applies,' he replied, mischievously taking advantage of her own embarrassment, forgetting everything else in the deliciousness of the moment. As a convent-bred miss of sixteen hearing her first compliment, Pernelle held down her head now. He was impressing, subduing, winning this first, last love of his life.

'There is a bond between us,' he went on smilingly, no longer himself, overcome by the sweetness of his triumph. 'I know your errand here: it is to pay down ready money for my last bit of land, to prevent me from starving. Supposing the tables turned, such service rendered you by a noble marquis would not alter our relations at all; your curtseyed thanks, and the world would be the same to both! But your hand'—his voice faltered with passion—'your beautiful hand held out to me, your unbidden kindness, accord the right to adore.'

'Let us not dwell on ourselves,' Pernelle said. 'The time is too solemn.'

'Should I dare to speak out at any other?' he cried. 'Shall I wait till—till we are both empty shadows, mere names to those who knew us here? But let me not look so far ahead, rather think of you as you are, imagine you ever the same. That is best. For my part'—

On a sudden he stopped short, listened, looked. Pernelle uttered a little cry of alarm.

The scene before them had changed in a moment. Fortuné's bombastic utterances were lost in prevailing clamour. Immediately around the auctioneer's stand all was uproar and confusion; three figures were seen struggling vainly for right of place. Above yells, shouts, and threats, the two listeners caught a watchword—

'Down with mainmorte! down with the law of the Dead Hand!'

Velours' presence of mind did not forsake him.

'You know La Fontaine by heart, without doubt,' he said, with the old cynical smile. 'If not, read the "Animals sick of the Plague," and think of me. But you must not stay here another instant. Coachman, quick, back to Dijon.'

With his own hand he turned the horse's head, then, bowing low, hastened to the rescue.

CHAPTER XXVII

'JE N'EN AVAIS NUL DROIT'

IN his immortal apologue the arch-fabulist recounts how the animals fell sick of the plague, how they assembled in conclave, one and all confessing their sins and offering himself as expiatory victim, with this proviso, that no worse offender could be found. We may all imagine what happened. The lion, who boldly admitted having gobbled up sheep at will, and occasionally the shepherd, was condoned, and the poor ass, who had only browsed on a foot or two of forbidden grass, was torn to pieces. But the fable does not suggest any foregone conclusion on the part of the deliberators, any long-nursed prejudice against the scapegoat. It was rather the occasion than the individual that demanded a sacrifice. Had no plague occurred, no disturbance of the existing order of things taken place, the donkey would have been left to his stolen mouthful of hay as the lion to his meal of sheep or shepherd.

La Fontaine knew human nature and human society regarded as a body politic too well to write otherwise, and represent men going out of their way for the summary administration of justice, holding up crimes that make looking-glasses of their own.

Perhaps no one present entertained a personal grudge against Louis de Velours. Many, with Fortuné, liked him, felt for him, as for some brother in misfortune; but he stood for more than one bad law, he represented centuries of tyranny and abuse of abominable privilege. His very appearance on the scene looked like an insult.

And alas, alas for human weakness! In the eyes of these poor people for the first time his poverty savoured of crime, affording excuse for violence and disdain. La Fontaine's grand fable was rehearsed with a vengeance, acted to the life on the human stage.

Velours' tall, attenuated figure, making calm way through the crowd, at first attracted no attention. No one expected him, and no one at the outset recognised him. Usually seen abroad in shabby shooting-dress, velveteen coat, leather gaiters, gun on shoulder, his present equipment served almost as a disguise.

It was his voice that betrayed, rather announced him. Speech divided noble and peasant hardly less than armorial bearings. Amid this tumult of rough oaths, coarse jokes, colloquialisms dark to the uninitiated, Velours' clear, correct utterance caught every ear.

'Neighbours,' he said, 'hands off these gentlemen, I command. A word with you all, then use me roughly if you please; only let my representatives alone.'

For a moment all stood still. The struggling auctioneer and his companions were unhanded; there was a brief pause. But one and all present were drunk, intoxicated with stimulant far deadlier than alcohol. Velours' very composure exasperated. No need to-day for a noble marquis to curse; he came of the class whose business had been to evoke curses. And of little use for him to command either! The year was just a week too old for that!

After the momentary hush came a derisive shout; again the functionaries pressed forward, still more roughly to be driven back. Fortuné, not at all divining Velours' errand, exulting in newly-acquired dignity and freedom, recommenced his tirade.

Very pale, and now with anger no less than alarm, the marquis entreated a second hearing.

'My good people,' he began, unable to hide his contempt, 'am I among reasonable beings or grown-up children, unable for a moment to control themselves? Let yonder gentlemen go, and listen to me. I have something weighty to communicate.'

'And so has he,' cried Pierre, pointing to the odd little figure on the rostrum. He entertained scant respect for a seigneur worse off than himself. 'Out with it, Fortuné, my man; we are all ears.'

Velours glanced round, and uttered an ejaculation of disgust. Not a gendarme was in sight, no emissary of the city police was there to whom he could appeal. His first impulse had been resistance, a firm stand against lawlessness and ruffianism. Seeing this hopeless, anxious at any cost to avoid violence, he now motioned the three officials to retire. The sale should not, of course, be persisted in; he had arrived at the eleventh hour to prevent it. But the first thing to consider was the safety of his friends.

With himself, these especial representatives of a bygone system were personally unobjectionable. They were known to be worthy, respected men. But no more than the marquis could they escape the odium of their status and profession. All four were intruders, offering wares for sale which belonged to others. Ignorant as they might be, these country folks knew something of seigneurial law. They had heard of seigneuries in which this horrible privilege of the Dead Hand did not hold good, in which a childless possessor had yet the right of willing away his own.

A show of yielding produced no good effect. The unresisting civilians were now as roughly prevented from retreating as a moment before they had been roughly driven back. What did the people want? To humiliate, to wreak vengeance? They hardly knew.

Velours grew desperate.

'Jeanne, my good friend Pierre, my honest father Robert,' he cried, 'do you not see what will, what must be, the result of such conduct?

There is still law in France. For Heaven's sake, interfere! let these gentlemen go. Fortuné,' he shouted, 'you at least will listen to me.'

As well address the winds! The ex-poacher and smuggler had no wish to harm any one, but he was beside himself with tickled vanity; for the first time in his life, too, he felt the consciousness of moral strength; for the first time he felt a man, free to speak, act, enforce his opinion.

'My good little Monsieur le Marquis, my excellent comrade,' he said, with the unctuousness of one in his cups, 'not for worlds would I displease you. Have we not been boon companions, ay, and more, for thirty years past? Had justice reigned in France, would noble marquises have escaped the pillory and the king's galleys more than poor smugglers and poachers like myself? No offence. Our pinch of tobacco, our barrel of salt, who is the worse to-day? And look out, my good Monsieur le Marquis; get what you can in the general scramble.'

That reference to his poverty, his associates, his connivance, certain illegalities to which he had been accessory, stung Velours to the quick;

but he was too much of a cynic, and also of an aristocrat, to waste temper upon such an audience. Underlying his sense of affront, moreover, was the conviction that these good people had right on their side. Was not their resistance justifiable; even Fortuné's familiarity but too well merited? Looking back, he could hardly blame himself; but the truth remained. His career had been ignoble, a vista to blush at. Bent now only upon averting excess, perhaps bloodshed, he did the brave, as he hoped, beneficent thing. Humiliating himself to the dust, he blurted out the truth.

'Neighbours,' he said, not a trace of passion in look or voice, for a moment his clear utterances subduing Fortuné's loud tones, 'a word— one word only. The sale shall not take place. I came hither to say so, to renounce my claim, and own the injustice of mainmorte, the law of the Dead Hand'—

The renunciation that comes an hour too late wears the aspect of enforced surrender. To admit the injustice of a law by which one's self and one's forefathers have benefited, is to invite the popular verdict. Even in worse odour are then the discharged agents of such privilege.

No oil cast upon troubled waters was Velours' speech, rather a brand held to piled-up combustibles. Shouts of 'Down with mainmorte! Down with the law of the Dead Hand!' again rent the air. Blows now fell thick and fast upon the defenceless townsmen. Velours, throwing himself between them and their assailants, received no better treatment. Vainly did one or two interpose, among these the meek-voiced Douce and her tractable Félix. It was not the Marquis de Velours, his auctioneer, notary, and notary's clerk folks were maltreating, but feudality itself, represented by the hated law of the Dead Hand. Could any deserve a worse fate?

CHAPTER XXVIII

PRACTICAL HEROISM

PERNELLE had not driven a hundred yards before she countermanded the marquis's order. Alongside and in front were the vehicles of her friends, all making post haste to Dijon. Ensconced as she was, a precipitate descent being hazardous, she nevertheless sprang down, displaying the daintiest ankles in the world, white silk stockings embroidered with vermilion-coloured clocks, and shoes—was ever fair Dijonnaise ill shod?—of exquisite material and fit.

But the young mercer was not thinking of her foot-gear just then—indeed, she could hardly be said to think at all. With some highly endowed natures, presence of mind takes the place of deliberation. Turn her back upon danger, forsake-fellow men in peril? As soon would she have thought of fleeing from contagious sickness in her own home, or passing a fallen child on the highway.

Just ahead was the calêche of her neighbours, the cloth merchant and wholesale dealer in hardware, whilst far advanced were two other vehicles, their occupants of Pernelle's sex and calling, but in no humour for the heroic. What, indeed, could stout, middle-aged ladies do in such a fray? And although the recent incendiaries were imputed to bands of miscreants, rather than these peasants, no one knew the exact truth. Clearly it was their first duty to take care of themselves—and their Sunday clothes! Busy middle-class women seldom went so far from home, and never without making elaborate toilette.

Pernelle bade the merchants' driver halt, and herself opened the carriage door.

'Gentlemen, my good friends,' she cried, 'there is not a second to lose. Pray alight and go with me. We are no strangers to yonder poor people. They may listen to us!'

The pair inside looked at each other and never stirred. She stood resolute, inviting, nay, commanding them to descend.

'Mademoiselle,' began the clothier—seniority of years, extra bulk and stature, larger business concerns, accorded right of precedence—'were I a younger man, a bachelor—above all things, were I of less unwieldy proportions—I would not hesitate an instant. Alas! obesity forbids Quixotism!'

'But not humanity,' Pernelle added vehemently; tears of indignation and distress were on her cheek, her voice trembled. 'Will you stand by and see your fellow-citizens maltreated, hounded down, perhaps killed?'

'Softly, softly, my dear young lady,' put in the hardwareman. 'I hope you don't regard our peasants as assassins? Those fine gentlemen yonder can do more for themselves than we can for them. And, like my good friend here, I, alas! have an impediment'—as he spoke he glanced down at his Falstaffian proportions. 'A blow in the stomach—excuse me, mademoiselle—is no joke when a man weighs fourteen stone, and will never see fifty-five again. The noble marquis and his men are slender and nimble as schoolboys. Trust them to get out of the scrape.'

'Will you drive away and leave me to

interfere alone on their behalf? Ah, a man is down!—it is the marquis himself!'

Uttering no syllable more, she left them, making what haste she could to the scene of conflict.

Her fellow-townsmen, turning very red, looked after her, then at each other. The hardwareman raised himself from his seat, and very reluctantly and deliberately stepped out.

'I would as soon venture on to a battlefield,' he murmured; 'but the girl is right, we are bound at least to show ourselves.'

Still more slowly and circumspectly the other set foot on the upper step, next with great care he folded a white silk handkerchief round his neck—in moments of peril, a Frenchman never forgets his muffler. Lastly, he alighted, indulged in a pinch, passing the snuff-box to his neighbour.

'We had better take our walking-sticks,' said the clothier.

'Show fight with such rotundities as ours?' was the retort. 'As well might a fat slug challenge a dragon-fly! No, no, moral force only for the like of us!'

Whilst moral force went on all-fours, might needed no spur.

The two worthy merchants, each having a cloak on his arm, as if indeed a scrimmage implied bad weather, had hardly made a dozen paces by the time Pernelle was close to the vineyard.

'Mademoiselle! my dear young lady!' they shouted, but she hastened on. There was command in the very tap of her high heels, dauntlessness in the adjustment of her pretty bonnet. Nor was it the first time that this girl of twenty-two had quelled a mutiny, of domestic kind, it is true, but none the less requiring courage and promptitude.

'Mademoiselle Pernelle!' repeated one Frenchman. 'Prudence above all things.'

'You, a husband and father, spend your breath on warning a woman!' added the second. 'I should have thought that by this time you knew better. The dear creatures would like nothing better than to storm a Bastille every day of their lives.'

Fortunately Pernelle had nothing of the tragedy queen about her; she represented the popular ideal, consummate business woman, just, if somewhat rigorous employer, and she was learned, could deal with facts and contracts like a notary, with books like a curé. She had been everywhere, that is, to Lyons, Marseilles, Paris, her experience counting as much as her taste. No stalls could vie with her own in made-up millinery, whilst for christening robes, confirmation caps, veils, scarves, and bridal coifs, she also stood first. Whenever a village beauty was about to wed, her finery, no matter on how small a scale, came from the 'Coiffe à Merveille.' Born democrat before democracy floated in the air, she encouraged such rustic custom, made the country folks feel at home with her, fitted them, suited their fancy as if they were great ladies. Her manner would be abrupt, slightly contemptuous, always domineering. This they relished. Such reputation served Pernelle in good stead to-day.

Affairs speedily took a serio-comic turn. With as little ado as if she were quieting some domestic insurrection, she now made her way. By an adroit wave of one hand, heavy Jeanne was sent a-flying; as unceremoniously by the other, Pierre's arm was pinched till he cried for mercy. A smart box on the ear brought the nearest stone-thrower to his senses. Two burly fellows, harmless as lambs till yesterday, but now bent on mischief, fell back under her scathing glance and merciless rating. No sooner did Fortuné catch sight of his enraged benefactress, than he slid from his stand with swift, lizard-like movement and hid himself behind others. From one end of the crowd to the other were heard low, disconcerted cries—

'Mademoiselle Pernelle!—it is Mademoiselle Pernelle!'

It was less her audacity, her fearless interposition, than the sudden appeal to reason, that wrought miracles now. Here incarnate was homely common sense, self-preservation, the fitness of things.

Not a rioter present but would have taken to his heels had flight been possible. Hemmed in between cabin and vineyard, forming a compact phalanx, all stood abashed, sheepish as penned flock awaiting the shearer.

'Must I call out all the gendarmerie of Dijon?' she cried, in that far-reaching, conscience-smiting voice her underlings knew so well. 'Must I blush, turn my back, pretend not to see you when next you want goods of mine? Men unworthy of the name, women shaming the titles of wife and mother, ask your patron saints and confessor for pardon—not me. Bear up yonder gentlemen. Make way for Monsieur le Marquis!'

'I don't think Monsieur le Marquis is hurt much, mademoiselle; and I hope you will bear witness to it,' whimpered Jeanne, apron to her eyes, 'neither Pierre nor myself have lifted a finger against those townsfolk!'

'And how many on their behalf, pray?' was the biting answer. Pernelle knew her people well. Lackadaisical appeal, mild entreaty, were here out of place. A sound rating is ever the best argument with ignorant misdoers.

'Fall back, every one of you,' Pernelle continued in the same short, sharp manner, surprising the most mutinous into passive obedience. 'Félix, Douce, you here? I should not have expected it! Fetch water from yonder spring. Fortuné, must you ever be by when mischief is brewing? Run as fast as your legs can carry you to the presbytery for linen and cordials. Are you indeed hurt, Monsieur le Marquis?' she added, motioning forward her neighbours the clothier and hardwareman. Meantime the three functionaries had shaken themselves, and although presenting a rueful appearance enough, were not seriously injured. Battered hats, torn garments, scratched and bleeding faces, and one or two ugly bruises, bore witness to the nature of their escape, and, as they now morosely said to each other, would furnish an ample report for the police.

But Velours was less fortunate. He had fallen, or rather been flung down, the entire weight of his body and of his assailant pressing upon one arm; as they helped him to rise, it fell helplessly by his side.

'La Fontaine's fable acted to the life,' he said, smiling despite sharp bodily anguish. 'I had no right to the vineyard—ah! mademoiselle, your hand'—

Some graver but less obvious injury had been incurred; only Pernelle's ready support prevented him from falling. The two merchants, who now came up, lent their aid, Douce and Félix helped as best they could. Soon Fortuné returned, bringing cordial and liniment, bandages and sponge; behind him, at a less rapid pace, following the parish priest. A brief consultation was held, then with all possible expedition they lifted the marquis into a carriage, and all three vehicles were driven back to Dijon. Meantime the crowd had dispersed as revellers caught in a thunderstorm. Only Fortuné, Douce, and Félix witnessed the departure.

'Humph!' said the foremost, shaking his head; 'I said all along how it would be.'

His companions walked home dumbfounded and crestfallen. They had no spirit to deny the assertion.

CHAPTER XXIX

THE COST OF REVOLUTION

'How mighty cross sister Pernelle has been of late,' said Barbe to Berthe one morning. 'She is perpetually vaunting this Revolution of hers. How much good has it done us, I should immensely like to know?'

Berthe answered with her hard little laugh.

'Shall I tell you what is going to happen? I peeped at sister's last letter to Uncle Parfait. "Business is so slack," she wrote, "that unless things soon mend, we shall all have to meet a crisis."'

'A crisis? What on earth does that mean?'

'That everybody in Dijon will have to shut up shop, ourselves included. Well, I for one should not cry.'

'I suppose we should live in the country, keep poultry, and make our own jam?'

'Much you know about it! A crisis means bankruptcy, and bankruptcy means having no money at all. But how delightful to get situations in Paris—see the Palais Royal and the Montgolfier balloon! I am sick to death of perpetually staring at Jacquemart and his wife, and hearing them strike the hours.'

Barbe reflected. Reflection was an accomplishment in which her twin was no adept. It did not seem to this astute little woman of sixteen that service even in Paris would offer unalloyed delight.

'And then,' continued Berthe, 'how dull to sit behind the counter from morning to night, without selling so much as a pair of garters!'

'Nobody has any money,' was the reply.

'What nonsense!' Berthe replied pettishly. 'People *must* have money, because they cannot do without it. But here comes Pernelle. Let us knit away.'

Time and the clock stay not for Revolution. To the quick, impetuous Dijonnais, it seemed as if their Fleming on Nôtre Dame raised his bâton at shorter intervals than before. Years rolled on, seasons sped, hours and days glided by, one and all indelibly marked in history.

Just twelve months after the delirium of liberty had come the delirium of brotherhood, an ebullition of humanity following an ebullition of justice.

On the Fourth of August of one year was pronounced the famous Declaration of the Rights of Man — Magna Charta, Habeas Corpus, and Petition of Rights, now for the first time become law in France. On the second great Fourteenth of July took place the Fête of Federation.

·For the first, and, alas! as yet only time in French history, traditions of caste and creed were set at naught. Noble and serf of yesterday fraternised as brethren. Tonsured priest and married pastor exchanged apostolic kiss, even assisted at each other's ritual. For a brief spell, a day only, all France became one. Before the sacred image of liberty—Isis at last unveiled—a magnanimous people forgot its injuries.

Meantime, amid the feverish outbursts of joy and shock of conflicting passions, humdrum folks, whose business it is to toil afield, in workshop or under ground, to traffic on marketplace or behind counter, went its usual way. Nor, at the onset, could these tremendous changes render bread-winning easier. On the contrary, such an upheaval naturally entailed confusion and loss. No revolution can be accomplished by half-a-dozen solemn gentlemen in black, seated round a table covered with green baize. Least of all could red tape effect the one great Revolution of history. The Upas that had overshadowed a nation, breathing deadliest poison, was felled, uprooted. Its branches no longer obscured the heavens, its roots no longer sucked the very life of the soil. But, far and wide, maleficent influences retained vitality, impeding healthful growth, diffusing germs of evil. Stout-hearted, confident, France went forth as a sower to sow. The good seed for awhile must fall on stony places.

For the first time Pernelle Nesmond confronted that hardest of all ordeals to an energetic nature, gradually slackened trade, an almost total cessation of business. After the Tricolour harvest came a long period of inertia. The world of fashion and frivolity was on the move. Adherents to the old order of things were fast crossing the sea or the frontier. Middle-class folks fêted domestic ceremonial with the least possible outlay. The peasants hid their gold pieces, awaiting the purchase of land. When Pernelle had written thus forebodingly to her uncle, it was of all Dijon, all shopkeeping France, rather than of herself. The national prospects were indeed gloomy—famine in one province, civil war in another, an empty treasury for the new government to fill as best it could, on all sides, bankruptcy or impending ruin. The accumulated debts of centuries, moral, social, material obligations, stared these new rulers in the face.

In her pretty bed-chamber, that also did duty for counting-house and reception-room, Pernelle sat over day-book and ledger. With that extraordinary alertness and grasp characterising French business women, she cast up column after column, added, deducted, verified, amid circumstances that would have driven others mad, not in the least put out by constant interruption.

Now Barbe would fling open the door with a customer's pattern of ribbon or lace and the nearest match in stock. Could Pernelle promise an exact counterpart from Paris or Lyons, and how soon? Next the maid-of-all-work would appear, huge basket in hand. Housekeeping then, as now, was carried on by daily marketings. Did mademoiselle wish for freshwater crabs? they were now to be had cheap; and salmon trout, too, was plentiful. A dozen questions were asked and answered before the good woman took up her basket. Then Berthe would burst in—Berthe was perpetually finding excuses for a run—she wanted beeswax for her stitching, might she run into the Rue Guillaume and fetch a lump; also for a feather broom, the last had come to pieces?

Meantime the auditing advanced. Pen in hand, Pernelle looked up, listened, deliberated, returning to her figures exactly at the point at which she had left off. Not a centime was miscalculated, not a date or entry confused. Nor did the young mercer show impatience or irritation; she was accustomed to do so many things at once!

In the midst of her task Laurent entered.

'Can I speak to you, cousin Pernelle?' he asked, in his habitually cold, hard way, the manner of a servant to just but unloved employer.

'Certainly. Sit down.'

'I interrupt, I see,' was the disconcerted, almost sullen response.

'Not at all—rather I should say I am used to being interrupted. You know how it is, I have never a second to myself.'

'Perhaps you will be freer towards evening?'

'That is extremely improbable,' Pernelle said, her pen fast moving as she spoke, her exquisitely neat, charming features bent over the huge ledger.

Laurent sat down moodily. Must it be ever thus with Pernelle and himself? Alike her courtesies and her benefactions affronted. He had come on the hardest errand a man could undertake, to humble himself in the dust before this adorable, hateful creature; and her condescension went no further than odd moments, intervals stolen between columns of day-book and ledger? Laurent Nesmond had grown, developed with the years and Revolution. No haughty stripling now awaited this audience of his benefactress and would-be protecting genius. Many things concurred to make the young man very humble, and at the same time very proud. The Fourth of August had placed him, with every other Nonconformist, on the footing of the orthodox. For the first time in history, Jew and African also enjoyed civil and religious rights. Nor was that all. Laurent's little patrimony, confiscated by the ever accursed Revocation, was to be restored, the consequences as well as the stigma of outlawry thereby annulled.

Again, as a tradesman his position had undergone a radical change. With feodality had fallen a system equally hampering and mischievous, that of trade guilds and corporations. A shopkeeper or artisan could now set up where he liked, and conduct business according to the method that best suited him. He was no longer bound hand and foot by laws and regulations that paralysed rather than stimulated industrial enterprise. The tyranny of capital did not survive the tyranny of rank.

But such blessings left the young man lonely, embittered as before. In some respects he owned to himself that his character had deteriorated; he was growing worldly, indifferent, ready for a future in which the heart hardly counted. Worldliness, indifference, had their advantage just now.

'Well?' said Pernelle, glancing up as she turned a leaf of her heavy duodecimo and drew the volume nearer.

'Well?'

CHAPTER XXX

LOVER AND LEDGER

THAT matter-of-fact 'Well?' brought a still colder, drearier expression into Laurent's face. He watched the beautiful accountant for a moment, smiling somewhat bitterly, then began.

'I have a long story to tell, my cousin. Have you patience to listen?'

'Go on; never fear that I shall lose a syllable, or'—hindered by the necessity of holding pen in mouth, she now finished her sentence—'that I will answer carelessly, supposing you have come for my opinion or advice.'

In no gaysome humour, Laurent nevertheless laughed aloud. 'I have come for something more important still. However, what matters? I see that you can quite well do two things at once—look over your accounts and at the same time receive a proposal of marriage.'

The irony of the situation came home to him. He thought sorrowfully that sentiment, even affectionateness, would have been more out of place.

Lead-pencils and blotting-paper were as yet unknown luxuries. Drenching her figures with the sand-box, Pernelle answered without looking up—

'Although my kinsman, you are hardly the person to be charged with such an embassy.'

There was no vexation, only surprise in her voice. Marriages were usually arranged through the medium of friends or relations. But the business should be undertaken with the utmost circumspection, the intervener should have social weight, experience, the authority of years.

'Pray do not misunderstand me,' Laurent put in very quickly. 'Not for worlds should I have taken the liberty of pleading for another. If I venture to do so for myself, it is because I have no advocate.'

Away went Pernelle's pen, swiftly moved eyes and lips as she checked another column of figures, then, still holding the page, she made reply.

'My poor Laurent, are these days for betrothal and marriage? You see how minutely I am going over my books. The year's profits have apparently fallen to zero.'

It was characteristic of Pernelle that she kept to the main issue, at once bent her mind to the present.

The past, in so far as it regarded Laurent and herself, was straightway banished from memory. He had unwillingly offered a cruel slight, he had indulged in a foolish, even unworthy romance. But, from first to last, his conduct was manly and dignified. No stain rested on his honour; and instead of the poor apprentice, the dependent, the outlaw, a man stood before her of comely, dignified presence, whose future, she felt sure, would shame no woman.

'Is not that rather an argument for me to put forward?' Laurent replied, for the first time feeling unready of speech, aggrieved at her own composure. 'Let me go back a little, my cousin, recall certain circumstances you seem to have forgotten.'

'Half a minute—in half a minute I am at your service,' Pernelle said, pen and lips moving more rapidly than before. 'Three thousand livres, five sols. Now go on.'

The sum-total was carried over, a leaf turned, then another column taken in hand.

'You have been the providence of me and mine,' he began.

'Four thousand livres, one sol — no, three sols.—Nonsense, Laurent, I but did my duty.'

Now, he hardly knew why, irritated by her whispered calculations and swiftly-moving pen, he continued—

'To-day I but do my own in endeavouring to repay the debt. I see that I can at last serve you; that in these troublous times even my poor name and protection may prove useful. You spoke of unprofitable seasons. You have of course heard that we Protestants are to be reinstated in our former possessions or indemnified by grants of money. Let my paternal heritage go, and the sum I receive instead, help to swell your capital, to compensate for your losses.'

Pernelle did at last momentarily pause in her auditing. A look of anguish stole over her face, she seemed on the point of tears. Had he at last touched her?

'You see how it is, Laurent. We cannot let our country-people starve, still less our country be handed over to a foreign despoiler. I have perhaps been too heedless in giving, not sufficiently mindful of the future; and meantime the rich, the spending class, have left France to perish, with their wealth are hiring mercenaries to crush her. Oh, poor France! Let us not talk of it.'

She returned to her figures, voice and expression indifferent as before. Laurent's countenance fell. Not on his account had she testified momentary weakness.

'The thought is generous. But you would feel the renunciation of your patrimony,' she said. 'Hard to regain one day and forfeit the next!'

Laurent's eyes grew dim with tears. His thoughts went back to a certain May day, when, by Finette's side, he had yearned for this good fortune, now come too late. How well he remembered his own words—'My little patrimony restored, wealth for us both!' But Finette had faded from his life as a dream; better to fix his mind on actualities and such consolations as they might afford, an honourable position, a worthy alliance, above all, the consciousness of having atoned for wrong. He knew it well enough—a girl of Pernelle's high spirit must feel the unintended slight he had put upon her.

'You speak of a trifling sacrifice,' he said. 'And—excuse me for the allusion, it is the last I will ever utter—I ought to have fallen in with your generous project from the first.'

'Seven thousand five hundred livres to balance against eight thousand. Talk of anything else, Laurent—forget that episode, if you please,' Pernelle exclaimed, with warmth and a slight accession of colour—Frenchwomen never blush. 'At any rate, we will decide for once and for all, that it is no argument against the step you now propose, and '—

Away went pen, fast as lips could move figures were gabbled over; the margin reached, her sum-total carried forward, she added—

'There leave it. You cannot think the worse of me for my proposal; I must respect your motive for having drawn back.'

'Have you nearly got to the end of your summing?' asked the young man, with some show of impatience.

These betrothals were as unromantic as could well be, the projected marriage was essentially one of expediency, but alike betrothals and marriage were his own. Dislike of Pernelle had long ago yielded before her serene forbearance; unswerving kindness and generosity had won him over in spite of himself. Love, passion, were out of the question; he did, however, expect a little feminine sympathy, some change of manner, if not of feeling.

Once more vigorously plying the sand-box, Pernelle turned a fresh leaf, then for a moment leaned back in her chair.

'I have got far enough to see that we have an uphill task before us, my poor Laurent, although, that I feel sure of, our affairs are in a much better condition than those of our neighbours.'

The exquisitely neat head was again bent down, and, pen in mouth, she rapidly scanned the open page.

'I will call to-morrow, or later on to-day, when you have made up your books,' Laurent said. There was a touch of sarcasm in his voice as he added, 'You must at least find a little more time for the notary.'

'Are you really going? Look in on Sunday at dinner, then. And do please write to Uncle Parfait. The news will indeed delight him. But I forget, he will be here soon.'

Laurent rose, made for the door, waited hesitatingly, at last returned to Pernelle's writing-table. In his loneliness and craving for affection, he felt such indifference keenly. Was she benevolence itself, yet without heart, pitiful in the extreme, but cold as ice? Would domestic life be bearable upon these terms?

'May I then regard the matter as settled— consider myself your future partner, in life as well as in business?'

'Dear, good Laurent, I am sure we shall be able to help, support each other through varying fortunes. And you have ever exercised authority over Berthe and Barbe. Henceforth I shall hand them over to you.'

Laurent smiled, although in no smiling humour. Pernelle was indeed taking him at his word, acknowledging him her partner of the fireside as well as counting-house.

'In all things your wishes are commands,' was the half-playful, half-serious answer. 'Adieu, then, till Sunday.'

Pernelle was rapidly lisping out another column of figures.

'Adieu,' she replied; then, pen between pretty lips, with both hands she readjusted her ledger.

'Nay,' he said teasingly,—had he not now the right to tease?—'the bond must be sealed.'

Stooping down, he claimed a bridegroom's kiss, and willingly enough she gave it, but without rising, without so much as taking the pen from her mouth. The captivating head was just held up, the beautiful forehead raised within reach of his lips. That was all.

CHAPTER XXXI

LOVE

Hardly had Laurent's tall figure passed out, than another presented itself, this time that of a stranger. So at least the young mercer concluded. Some silk merchant from Lyons or ribbon manufacturer from St. Etienne had come for orders, or, Heaven help them! for the accommodation of a loan.

At this period, business men and women thus stood by each other, the least unprosperous helping their friends.

'A moment—in a moment, citizen, I am at your service,' Pernelle said, without rising; she was half-way through a new column of figures. 'Pray be seated.'

The new-comer obeyed, first having assured himself that this charming room, counting-house, boudoir, and maiden's bed-chamber in one, was quite safe from espiers and eavesdroppers.

With a resounding clap that made her visitor jump from his seat, Pernelle shut ponderous ledger; as a second report came the closing of no less ponderous day-book. Then the young mistress of the ' Coiffe à Merveille ' rose to salute her client. He rose also, and stood bareheaded, bending low.

The attitude betrayed him. No fellow-tradesman would have greeted her thus ceremoniously. A cheery 'how d'ye do' ever preceded business overtures, whatever their nature.

'Monsieur le Marquis!' she cried, dropping into a chair. The door had not only closed upon Laurent, it had closed upon the world of every day.

'There are no longer marquises in France —have you forgotten?' he said, smiling sadly. ' My marquisate, which was indeed but a name, disappeared on the Fourth of August two years and more ago, the day on which you saved my life and other lives more worth the saving.'

'I but exercised a little common sense. I

think any woman would have done the same,' she replied.

'You risked your own safety—there is something more than mere common sense in that,' was the reply, Velours looking at her adoringly, wistfully as he spoke. Oh, if this conversation might be renewed to-morrow, and to-morrow, and to-morrow! his face said.

'I have longed for news of you,' Pernelle continued, the absolute genuineness, the uncompromising sincerity, the legitimate manliness, so to speak, of a brave woman's nature never for a moment forsaking her. 'Once I did see Father Albin, he told me of your recovery, that was all. I wanted to know more.'

A flush of pleasure on Velours' face was followed by an expression of deep, self-pitying anguish. She 'longed for news of him, to know more,' and every word he had to say for himself must open a gulf of separation.

'Monsieur le Marquis'—

'I am only Louis de Velours—Monsieur de Velours if it please you. To the new-fangled title of Citizen I lay no claim.'

All that she yearned to hear was disclosed

in a sentence! The slight contemptuousness of his utterance escaped her notice.

She sat dumbfounded, as one stricken with grief. Why should he stay a single moment longer? What more had they to say to each other?

'I have pained you?' he said, not with a look that asked for pardon, that pleaded excuse, rather with the air of one whose vindication was self-evident.

'And because I have pained you,' he went on, still proudly, almost defiantly confronting his listener, 'you are bound to hear me to the end. Much has happened since we last met. You may meantime have imagined me an unwilling convert to the new order of things— from my own point of view, a renegade. It is not so. But never for an instant deem that I have not weighed matters, reflected on them, kept anxious vigils, done all that in me lay to discern the biddings of conscience. Can the great and the wise aver more—from one point of view, as much?'

He seemed to attain even added stature, certainly more nobleness of face and figure, whilst thus pleading for himself. But Pernelle did not see, had no need to see. His voice told her all.

'These past two years have been one perpetual struggle. Was ever a man's existence so pitiful as mine, his soul, his conscience, of such small account? And how easy to invent sophistries! Why set my own poor judgment against that of the people and their leaders, such men as sit at Versailles, such women as yourself! Should not the collective conviction of many stand before the opinions—prejudices in your eyes—of the few? Again and again I have said Yes, have even started on the way'—

He moved nearer, caught her unresisting hands to his lips, and sobbed out—

'On the way to you. No other goal beckoned, no other path invited. I only wanted to see you once more, to tell you that I was yours, heart, soul, the last drop of blood devoted to your cause, at last, made my own. This joy might not be.'

Drawing back, tacitly asking pardon for his outburst, he added—

'Plead if you will, torture—or shall I say, enrapture?—me with womanly appeal.

Clasp my knees, weep over my hands as just now I wept over your own, entreat, persuade, promise—I must not — I dare not yield.'

Pernelle looked at him for a moment, speechless with sorrow.

'I am less than nothing,' she got out at last. 'Why speak of ourselves at all?'

Steadying her voice by an effort, she went on—

'The sufferings of the people, do not these speak, thousand-tongued? But of what good to say more? Indeed'—here a tone of the self-composed, matter-of-fact business woman wellnigh deceived him, undoing the sweet triumph of her momentary agitation—'indeed, Monsieur le Marquis, I am asking myself why you are here.'

Genuine passion is neither to be blinded nor resisted. Now for the first time Pernelle came within its influence, and his heart beat quickly at the thought. This girl's life had been devoted to buying and selling, perhaps sordid, if honest cares, her own individuality merged in family interests. At last a voice reached her—not the voice of patriotism, not the voice of duty, one wholly strange, undreamed of, disconcerting.

The feint over, she was herself again—the self that had come into being half an hour ago, the self that belonged to him.

'I will not forget you, I will try to think kindly of you,' she said, without looking up. 'Only go—we must not meet any more.'

'We shall not meet any more,' he said, settling himself in his chair, not even desperate circumstances robbing the moment of deliciousness. They were alone. She was tearful, heart-broken, troubled, and all on his account. He sat, drinking in the sight of her, as men condemned to the scaffold drink in the last breath of heaven.

'You are bound to the frontier or to Vendée?' she cried, with a look of abhorrence —'to swell the invading hosts or that crueller foe nursed on French soil? You will shed the blood of your brethren, overthrow their hardly-won liberties, place your country under the heel of the foreigner?'

'It rests with yourself,' he said, once more a lover's triumph in his eyes. 'You cannot make me turn traitor to conscience, but you can prevent me from finally redeeming a wasted life. You are my destiny whether you will or no.'

He waited, thinking she would guess the rest.

Pernelle remained irresponsive.

'And the only friend I have in the world who can help me now, help me to the poor satisfaction I speak of'—

His voice faltered, and once more tears dimmed his eyes.

'Life is emptiness, the grave, silence, but the name a man leaves behind him is something real, something the meanest must take account of. I shall most likely die by a sword-thrust, or be shot as a traitor with my back to the wall. You may never learn the truth. Years hence, make up your mind that it has been so, and rejoice that a good-for-nothing life ended in honourable death. The cause, dear'— He held her hands tight. Both were weeping.

'Why trouble ourselves about the cause? Suffice it that I deem my own a righteous one. Thus I place myself on your level too. You will not refuse?'

'You have come to me for a passport?' she asked, through her tears.

It was well known that Deputy Nesmond's niece had helped more than one frightened, insignificant client out of the country. Thousands who might have remained in perfect safety daily flocked towards the border, those who were in duty bound to remain, whose mere presence guaranteed the safety of others, leading the van.

Velours' case wholly differed from any hitherto brought under Pernelle's notice.

Poltroonery, self-interest, clinging to worldly fortune, had actuated former petitioners. This suppliant asked at her hands privilege of other kind, freedom to follow conscience—in other words, a sentence of death.

He bowed assent to her question. She rose hurriedly, unable to bear his presence any longer, for the first time in her life unnerved, disarmed, at the bidding of overmastering emotion.

'To-morrow—by noon—it shall be ready,' she got out, motioning him to go.

'If I could only wait till to-morrow!' he replied, not stirring an inch. Then, triumphant in the possession of a few blissful moments more, shrinking drearily from the thought his own words called up, he added—

'You forget that the Revolution has changed everything, even the march of Time. The present moment must stand for to-morrow.'

CHAPTER XXXII

THE STRUGGLE

WITH uncertain steps and trembling fingers Pernelle moved towards her escritoire and fitted key to the lock. Then, torn by cruellest conflict, she leaned back, covering her face with her hands.

'Vendée, Vendée!' she murmured, 'stepdaughter who would throttle our mother France, shall I, of all others, put a sword in thy traitorous hands, or, worse still, help to swell the army of mercenaries wooed to my country's, our country's, downfall?'

She confronted him tenderly, fearlessly, emboldened by mutual confidence, by the tie, intangible as gossamer, indissoluble as castiron, that bound them together. Affianced lovers could hardly feel nearer to each other, linked in closer bonds, than these two; for an hour, a moment, they were one, henceforth to be strangers.

'Say you will not join the Vendéans or the hired foes at Coblentz,' she pleaded. 'Think of what this civil war means, what this host of foreign invaders are bent upon. Your heart is French as well as mine; you have seen the sufferings of the people, the abasement of the kingdom. And if Vendée gets the upper hand, if Coblentz becomes the seat of government, everything will be a thousand times worse than before. The doom of France is irrevocably sealed. Cross the Manche, make free England your home. You will find many friends there; forget that you were born in France.'

'Could I forget that for a moment, I were all, more than you wish,' he said calmly and despondingly, his tone and manner in striking contrast with her own., Pernelle's impetuosity and forcibleness had their source in hope and in the assurance of a future. For him the life that was life indeed had already ended.

'Of what use to try and make things clear?' he went on. 'There are beliefs, principles, that we have sucked in with mothers' milk, that have become part of our very being. Do as you will, refuse the boon I ask, only leave me my conscience, the spark of loyalty that makes me worthy of you.'

He quitted his chair and moved to the escritoire. Bending low, he continued in undertones—

'Put back your keys; let me fare as best I may. I had no right to ask for the passport. Forget the request, forget everything concerning me; only in your turn expect not oblivion. And if I might only petition for a token! some little thing that you have used or worn, to carry away as priests their crucifix, pilgrims their holy relic.'

With a wistful glance his eye roved from coveted object to object, the little nothings at her watch-chain, the tiny mother-of-pearl brooch fastening her kerchief, the silk mittens on dainty wrists.

Pernelle hardly heard. Passionately bent on serving him, her mind was occupied with practical issues. His wasted past rose before her, apologising, pleading. Could she send him away, withholding the only boon he craved, means of making final peace with himself, of sacrificing life to what he regarded as duty?

On a sudden light flashed upon her. She saw a way out of the dilemma.

Once more she fitted key to the lock, and with quick, business-like movements drew forth the precious document, last of the free safe-conducts entrusted to her by Deputy Nesmond.

'Again and again and again you will be able to repay this service,' she began. 'I ought to have thought of it before. Vendée is merciless —no foreign foe so ruthless to the vanquished; Move the misguided peasants to pity. Recall the priests to a sense of Christian duty. We are French as well as you.'

The pretty head was bent low, away flew pen across paper, he sitting by, mechanically answering her questions.

'I think this is correct,' she said, when her task was ended. 'Please look over my entries.'

Yes, the passport was in order; so far the way lay clear. She now thought of another difficulty. How could she put the simple question—Do you want money? Her quick woman's eye discerned a tale of makeshift and poverty in his garments, of privation in his spareness. She noted, too, that although winter was at hand, he wore no cloak.

'Can I do anything else for you?' she asked, still curt and matter-of-fact. 'Any kindness, remember that, you can pay back with double and treble interest.'

He smiled sadly. Had she not given him two inestimable boons already, his face said; the life of feeling, which alone is life indeed, and a chance of moral redemption?

She took a little embroidered bag of gold pieces from the escritoire and pressed it upon him, folding his fingers over the treasure with her own.

'Take this as a token from me; the needlework is my own. It will serve as a keepsake; and with the money, minister to my wounded patriots, feed the widow and fatherless. Yet the offering is unconditional.'

Her voice faltered. Moving towards the door, grasping the handle, with face averted, she tacitly implored him to go, thanks unuttered, farewells unspoken.

But he could not be thus dismissed. They would never meet again; she must know all.

'Why should I not take your money? why should I waste a thought on your generosities?' he said. 'Pardon me if I seem to jest; think of my desperate case. The truth, then, is this. Revolution might mean to me, not a fatal skirmish in Vendée, or being shot with my back to the wall in Paris, but hope, joy, love! I have only to go over to your side, to make common cause with the people, and I might try to win, instead of a memory, yourself.'

She started. The thought had never once occurred to her mind.

'Think for a moment. I have already received overtures from Paris. My education, poor although it be, renders me valuable; and renegade nobles are in request. It is in my power to sink my former personality for once and for all, as plain Citizen Velours better my fortunes, fulfil an important, or at least respectable post, become, in worldly matters at least, and certainly in worldly eyes, a fitting suitor for the first bourgeoise of Dijon. My life is here, yet I cannot stay.'

Had the Fleming in the clouds struck an hour since that passionate utterance, his automatic spouse sounded the half, their bantling the quarter only? Or had the minute hand barely gone its round? To Pernelle's thinking time must have made a leap. She who had never considered the passing years from a feminine point of view, who knew no dread of whitening hairs or furrowing lines, found herself suddenly aged before her time; real youth, the immortal youthfulness of romance, burst into flower, withered, scattered to the winds, in an hour!

'And because I cannot stay, we are quits. You are free to offer benefactions; I may accept your generosities. My memory need not shame you, although linked with that of Vendée.'

'Niece, niece, who speaks of Vendée?' cried a cheery voice in the doorway, and there,.Berthe clinging to one arm, Barbe to the other, stood Uncle Parfait.

Pernelle sprang forward joyously, holding out both hands, for the moment forgetting everything in the delight of his presence. Not at first recognising each other, the two men merely bowed; then the armourer threw off his cloak, tossed a packet to each twin, with which they scampered away giggling, finally turned to hostess and guest.

'You are perhaps settling some business with yonder gentleman ; I intrude?' he asked, glancing from Pernelle to the tall figure standing with his back to the window, in the October twilight a mere silhouette. 'Yet what business can a niece of mine have with the accursed name of Vendée?'

CHAPTER XXXIII

— AND STRUGGLE

The last words recalled Pernelle to realities.

With lightning-like rapidity she grasped the problem suddenly placed before her, and bent her whole intellect to a solution. Only one was possible, the plain truth. No matter what the truth might cost her uncle, her lover, herself, it must be told unflinchingly. As swiftly had come revelation and inner debate to the other two.

In her hospitable welcome Pernelle's smouldering fire was not forgotten. The added log blazed up making every object clear. Velours and Nesmond, amicable buyer and seller of former days, now sworn to deadliest feud, stood face to face; between them, gage of contest, the free pass.

Velours might easily have availed himself of the other's sudden appearance to pocket his document and take quiet leave, thereby avoiding painfullest scene. On Pernelle's account he was already blaming himself for the bolder course.

But there was Revolution not only in the air; in men's blood too it germinated spontaneously; long before the greatest revolutionary had formulated its watchword — Daring — more daring—perpetual daring!—the spirit of fearless initiative possessed all classes.

Velours now revelled in the thought of vindicating himself before this bourgeois, proving that a poor, broken-down nobleman, formerly occupied in poaching with second-hand or antiquated weapons, was his match for courage and patriotism.

On the other hand, the armourer's first feeling was of reluctance. He shrank with disgust from the situation thus forced upon him. His hatred of the noblesse, now leagued against France and French liberties, was deep-rooted and intense. But he felt an honest man's respect for lifelong ties and business transactions. Many and many a time he had himself repaired Velours' ancestral flint-lock, the two chatting after friendliest fashion all the while.

Many a time, too, the marquis had accepted a glass of good wine in the back shop, ay, and an occasional feast of galettes to boot!

And this very man, this of all others, should ask favours of his niece, should trade upon former acquaintance for such a purpose? There was no need to ask his errand. The passport lay on the table. He had caught the word 'Vendée.'

The three glanced at each other: Pernelle sorrow-stricken but resolute—her word being given, duty was clear; Velours almost arrogant in his new position, lover, soldier, patriot; the armourer black-browed, menacing, his implacable mood plain without a word. It was characteristic of the three that each so entirely relied on the other's loyalty. What easier than for Pernelle or Velours to take up the passport, for Nesmond to throw it in the fire? Such an alternative never occurred to either; all awaited the full fury of the storm.

'Not accursed, oh, my uncle! Vendée is still France, French hearts beat there as in our own Bourgogne. Let us not curse, rather try to win them over.'

'Is it my niece whose voice I hear, whose

handwriting I read yonder, one of my own blood and name, who is sharpening another sword against our country?' cried the armourer, almost beside himself with dismay. 'Girl, hitherto my second self, what vile potions have you drunk, how comes it that your reason is thus disturbed? And you, sir,' he went on, turning to the marquis; 'surely it would better have become an honest gentleman to knock at any other door but that of an unprotected girl, head of a house, staff of orphan sisters'—

The taunt did not ruffle the other's calm. Velours had evidently prepared himself for harder hits, more piercing reproaches.

'Was it not enough,' continued Nesmond, 'that she rescued you from ruffianly assailants two years ago, conveyed you to a place of safety, sent Sisters of Mercy to minister to you? Must the rendering of one service, that wholly honourable, entail others, shameful in themselves, disastrous in their consequences? Relinquish all claim to that document, give up your so-called patriotism, and go back to your partridge-shooting. I will answer for your personal safety.'

Velours glanced at Pernelle. Her face said nothing, but he divined her thoughts.

'A free gift should ever be freely surrendered. But at the bidding of the giver only. Listen,' added the marquis proudly, taking up the safe-conduct as he spoke. 'Hear me, for a moment, monsieur—I beg your pardon, Citizen Nesmond. I have also a word to say. You alluded contemptuously to my former mode of existence just now, and no wonder. Was I wholly to blame for such sordidness and degradation? Were there not seigneurs as much victimised by the old state of things as any peasants could be? How was I to better my condition, rise in the social and moral scale, to say nothing of the material. Could a marquis earn honest bread, be admitted into one of your trade guilds and corporations? As surely as our quarters of nobility kept you out of our ranks and dignities, your rules and statutes prohibited us from attaining your own. But enough of recrimination on either side.' His tone changed from intense bitterness to hauteur and irony.

'My antecedents I cannot undo, but the future at least is mine. And your Revolution has rendered even a broken-down nobleman one service. It has aroused his patriotism.'

'Revolution, patriotism, forsooth!' put in the armourer, his voice rasping but controlled. He was by this time well inured to heated discussion. Instead of losing his temper to-day, he but showed more force and masterfulness. As he spoke his brow was a veritable thundercloud.

'You are right, Monsieur Velours, we have talked enough. No more blasphemy, I beg. Let us end this business. Will you take advantage of a girl's generosity, league yourself with traitors, become a hireling of the foreigner, help to enslave France, or will you not? That is the question, and the sooner answered the better—the better for all three.'

He turned to Pernelle, not a trace of the old adoring pride and fondness in his face, not a sign of compromise or yielding in his voice; it was no longer the maiden or darling appealed to, but one by force of judgment and will his equal.

'Remember,' he added, 'Vendée means one thing, and one thing only, civil war, foreign invasion, the crushing of French liberties. And remember also—did you ever know me break my word?—yonder paper means one thing only to you and to me.'

Pernelle did not for a moment lose self-possession. She understood but too well the cruel force of her uncle's words. He asked her to choose between the protector of her youth, the father, mother, friend in one, till lately her all, and a stranger, in a day, an hour, more than usurping his place. She was as far as ever from being guided by sentiment. In her utter loneliness and anguish she tried, as she had striven throughout life, to follow the upright, truthful, business - like course. To this high-minded yet mundane girl, conscience had been religion, other creeds touching her feebly.

'Uncle,' she cried, 'must my word be lightly broken either? And this gentleman may do our cause more good than harm, he may plead on the side of consideration, of humanity. He goes against us, but as an honourable foe.'

'Is that all you have to say?' asked Nesmond, taking up hat and cloak, evidently about to leave.

'A moment, dear uncle!—you are tearing my heart to pieces—a moment only!' she cried.

The armourer paused, but not at her bidding. With a quick movement Velours now sprang forward and tried to force the passport into Pernelle's hand.

'Too dear at such a price would be all the fine things I spoke of just now,' he said, his old cynicism come back. 'No, my good Monsieur Nesmond—I beg pardon—no, citizen, leave me my partridge-shooting, keep—keep'—the words 'your niece' were on his lips; suddenly cynical composure forsook him, his voice broke down.

Nesmond glanced at Pernelle sharply. There was no need for more than a glance, hardly that, indeed. Would she have been his brother's child, of his name and race, had she yielded?

The fonder his pride, the keener his grief. With a suppressed sob, never once looking back, the armourer drew his hat over his brows, gathered his things together, and passed out.

Velours followed slowly. He did not trust himself to speak; would words have meant anything at all? He did not venture to kiss her hand; silence, reserve, the enforced composure only tears must have broken, made all clear.

Pernelle understood better than the most

passionate outpourings could have told, how he left her to meet solitude ; with herself, with her uncle, and of his own free will, condemned to utter loneliness, loneliness only ending in the still more solemn loneliness beyond the tomb.

But she was not wholly unconsoled, nor were these two, of that she felt assured. 'Oh,' she murmured, covering her face with her hands, 'the cost of Liberty! The bitter price paid for an ideal!'

CHAPTER XXXIV

'AUX ARMES, AUX ARMES, CITOYENS!'

REVOLUTION was not a year older, yet the Fleming above Nôtre Dame seemed to have given out centuries rather than days, weeks, months since that stormy scene in Pernelle's little salon. What had happened, rather, what had not happened, in France meanwhile? Small wonder that the leading revolutionists were all young men and women—for women also helped to raise the structure of French liberties — carelessly flinging away life in their prime. White-haired sages, veterans wedded to routine and expediency, would never have steered the ship through such perilous seas.

As Minerva from the head of Zeus her sire, arose these youthful legislators, warriors, moral inventors, fully matured and equipped from parent soil. Time and the event were their only educators, such schooling having to be acquired in a day.

To secure great treasure is something; the crowning achievement, the superhuman task, is to retain it. A band of dauntless reformers had given their country her Magna Charta, had proclaimed to all the world the doctrine of absolute civil and religious equality. But to drive the foreign hordes from the frontier, to suppress the ever-swelling host of fanatics at home? The gifts now so sorely needed, generalship, strategy, the power of organising, were they also ready to hand? Would commanders, victors, spring up as the fabled giants from Jason's sowing?

Had Pernelle been any other but Pernelle, business might have fared badly during the last few months, Berthe and Barbe run wild as they pleased, all kinds of irregularities occurred. But no such thing. The young mistress of the Coiffe à Merveille never for a single moment let self stand before that thousandfold self called duty. Her manner had perhaps become a trifle brusquer, her voice had taken a more decisive tone, she showed less forbearance towards small shortcomings; whilst for her own part she wrought more assiduously alike in shop, counting-house, or kitchen. Like every other housewife, Pernelle superintended each branch of domestic economy in person, her vigilance never flagging. In one respect matters remained the same at the well-known sign. Its young mistress still reigned supreme, unwedded and alone.

'You see what is inevitable, dear Laurent,' she had said soon after the interview with Velours and her uncle. 'Civil war and foreign invasion are imminent. Every man's place will then be in the ranks. Better keep your freedom.'

In a less matter-of-fact tone she added—

'And there is another reason for delay, I cannot marry till I have made up this unhappy difference with my uncle. His blessing on our union I must have.'

Winter gives timely warning to the good citizens of Dijon, and it is prudently taken. Already in summer, folks begin to store their fuel, before each door being deposited timber to be cut up on the spot, or neatly-cut logs brought from St. Jean de Losne in barges, in carts and hand-trucks from neighbouring forest. Every street becomes animated with the woodman and his business, masters and matrons surveying their purchase, idlers gossiping as they gaze, drivers good-naturedly squabbling over right of way. From the Porte Guillaume to the Place d'Armes the scene was one of noise, bustle, and confusion. For the most part the wood was chopped at the buyer's door, the rhythmic fall of axe and chopper echoing far and wide. No one knew better than Pernelle the truth conveyed in La Fontaine's fable. The eye of the master can never be spared. Having ordered a truck of wood, she must, of course, supervise chopping and stowing away. Most Frenchwomen can do several things at once, and she was no exception to the rule. Keeping one eye upon her woodman, the other upon her stalls opposite, tripping gracefully to and fro, she was here, there, everywhere at once.

Now some worthy bourgeoise had to be suited with a Sunday cap, Pernelle turning her head this side and that as she tried one after another. Now Berthe was caught bungling over her work, or Barbe reading a newspaper. The twins out of sheer perversity had become ardent Royalists, and would fain have slipped off to Vendée and served in the rebel army as sutlers. Truth to tell, the minxes did not relish what may be called the sumptuary aspect of Revolution. What were the rights of citizens, representative government, just laws, to them? But to go short of gingerbread and berberries, to have no new frocks or bonnets from January to December, were grievances that touched them nearly. Evil times must be met, the shivering and hungry ministered to, patriotic needs aided, and only by means of the most uncompromising economy. Pernelle's rule was here Draconian. If Berthe pouted at the coarse rye bread, smelt it, eyed it, pretending she could not eat, her elder's answer was a curt—' Then go hungry.'

If Barbe declared that her Sunday gown disgraced the very church, she only got by way of consolation—

' Then go naked.'

The two talked of Vendée, dreamed of Vendée morning, noon, and night. There were moments when they seriously contemplated running away, and whenever Pernelle's back was turned, would talk of their plans, as they called them.

'Think of a cantinière's bewitching dress! how well the gold-braided coat, short skirt, and high boots would become me!' cried Berthe to-day; 'and to watch the balls flying on the scene of battle, and catch a handsome young officer mortally wounded in my arms. No, not mortally'—

'Why not?' coolly asked Barbe—she seemed to have no more moral sense than a butcher-bird. 'You would then get his watch and diamond ring.'

'I should prefer a kiss,' was the reply; 'and were he count or marquis, an offer of marriage.'

'Hark! do you hear drums beating?' cried Barbe.

The pair dropped their needlework and listened attentively. True enough, drum and tambour sounded, although as yet far off. But Berthe and Barbe would have detected the noise amid the fracas of an earthquake, the hurly-burly of a tornado. To these two it was irresistible as bugle-horn to hunter, tally-ho to hound.

'It is a recruiting party—sister said the recruiting was to begin,' said Barbe.

Heedless of the consequences, unmindful, perhaps vain, of displaying neatly stockinged, gaily gartered legs, away they flew, leaping timber, piled-up logs, and even chopping-block, overturning portable ovens of griddle-cake seller, now running against one sedate citizen, now another. Nothing could arrest their mad course at sound of the Rataplan.

Pernelle glanced after them for a moment with knit brows, then her face softened, glowed. She overlooked the offence in the occasion.

'The recruiting begins to-day, neighbour?' she asked of a portly fellow bourgeoise, with herself supervising the unloading and storage of wood, but, unlike Pernelle, no enthusiast in the cause of Revolution. The good woman could not conceive what soldiers had to do with the business. To her thinking, although democratic in principle, a monarchy was essential to French prosperity, but a monarchy well kept within bounds, *rois fainéants* trotted out once a year by way of upholding tradition, government transacted by notaries seated at a table covered with green baize.

'Recruiting to-day means widows and orphans to-morrow, and wood so dear that we shall have to chop up our linen presses and bedsteads, or go without dinner. No, Mademoiselle Pernelle, none of your Marseillaises for me!'

Pernelle's face saddened, a few minutes later to become radiant. No more than her neighbour could she forget the awful aspect of this appeal. Her heart bled for the young wives bereft of their bread-winners, the mothers taking last look of beardless darlings. So strongly did she feel the day's solemnity, that she determined not to visit the Place d'Armes. Better to calm herself over daily work, leaving others to acclaim the volunteers!

But the Marseillaise and the popular enthusiasm proved irresistible, she was borne away on the current against her will. Although only a few months old, the one great song of the world was now familiar to every man, woman, and child in France. No sooner did its moving strains reach Pernelle's ear, than she went indoors, unpinned her apron, and tripped to the end of the street; her buxom neighbour did the same, their woodmen followed, all Dijon was magnetised towards the recruiting booth as moths to a candle.

'I must have a peep! just a peep!' cried every one.

The butcher forgot to throw down his knife, the barber left his client half-shaven, the shoemaker rushed out last in hand, the baker emerged all floury from his oven, the apothecary was far too excited to leave pestle behind. Never surely had folks so forgotten decorum and prudence! What if ill-disposed loafers lurked about, pilferers, shop-lifters, professional thieves?

None paused to think. The Marseillaise was as 'that song the sirens sang,' only wax-stopped ears could resist. Once more people were drunk, but not with wine. As drum beat, tambour sounded, and from hundreds and thousands of voices rose the strain—

> 'Aux armes, aux armes, citoyens,
> Formez vos bataillons!'

the new force of France, the patriotic army that was to re-create the mother country, the land of Jeanne d'Arc, came into being, was formed as by magic. At the self-same hour and in the same magic fashion, from mountain and plain, sea-coast and valley, from counting-house and manor, workshop and hovel, sprang untried but dauntless defenders of French liberty, founders of the Republic!

CHAPTER XXXV

THE TOCSIN

BUT two voices were now making themselves heard throughout the length and breadth of France, with the clarion note of hope alternating the knell of despair. Which would die away and be forgotten? by which would the great gods speak—the Marseillaise heralding victory, the Tocsin presageful of doom?

Now the one seemed uppermost, and now the other: for awhile spirits were cheered, uplifted; for awhile men deemed that the end of the world, of their France, was near. 'The mother country in danger!' Such was the signal thundered from a thousand brazen mouths; by way of answer came the noblest martial air that ever cheered on to glory. It was natural and fitting that the first should dominate. Warning less awful, appeal less stringent, would have proved vain. A voice must resound from one end of France to the other, bringing the stoutest-hearted to their knees, as children before an awful storm.

The Tocsin, thousand-tongued, drenching the country with terrifying sound, seemed no simultaneous clanging of myriad watch-bells, instead, a letting loose of retributive spirits, ministers of divine visitation.

So, indeed, the simpler peasant folk regarded the matter, only by slow degrees brought to understand its meaning.

Their country was in danger, her very existence as a nation threatened. By one means alone could France be saved—the voluntary sacrifice of her children.

The Tocsin warned of deadly peril, the Marseillaise announced delivery.

Where did those dread carillons begin? Whence were first echoed back those dreadful chimes? Folks woke up to hear on a sudden. It was as if some magic touch had set all the alarums in France going at once. None could think of sweating bell-ringers in high, cobwebby towers, of steaming brows and swollen muscles, of many a copious wine-draught between pull and pull, and oath, to boot—the toil was tremendous, but well paid, and should not be wasted! To-morrow and to-morrow the ropes should be tugged, ay, and, by the Blessed Virgin, harder than ever! The Tocsin was not only rung for France to hear, but for the ears of her enemies, of all Europe!

From Marseilles the awful peal rang forth, reaching the rocky shore and umber islets set in sleepy blue sea. The red-capped, mahogany-complexioned fisherman heard far away, and on a sudden his lateen sail moved, the little craft, hitherto motionless as burning heaven above, made with all speed for the harbour.

High above the terraced city, vine-dressers, thinly clad as Orientals, toiled between glistening white walls and golden leafage. One and all, they too threw down pruning-knife and hoe, hastening to learn the news, mixing in the tumultuous crowds below, returning to the vineyard no more, within an hour enrolled as volunteers. From city to city, townling to townling, hamlet to hamlet, the torrential stream of sound was maintained without a break; as those beacon fires blazing from Troy to Argus kept up a chain of blazing lights, so each peal was now caught ere its fellow died away.

Through the olive groves and peach orchards of hot Provence, silvery-green wavelets, fruitage dazzling as those of Aladdin's garden—by the crocus-coloured walls and sapphire sky of Aigues-Mortes, the Tocsin passed, not for a moment interrupted by the broad blue Garonne nor the mountain fastnesses of the Pyrenees. Above tinkling cattle bell and musical little river, above war of cascade and wind surging among the giant pines, the sound rolled on; it leaped from spire to spire perched above hanging pastures under snow-capped peaks, penetrated cool valleys beneath the awful shadow of Gavarnie, echoed along the pale brown measureless wastes of Gascoigne.

The stilted shepherd made what haste he could to the nearest village, finding there the same ferment that reigned in capitals, henceforward shepherd no longer; on a sudden become patriot, soldier!

From the grand belfry tower of Bordeaux, the watch-bell rang forth a deafening peal; by mile upon mile of wharfage it ran, by noble harbour bristling with a thousand masts, to the hither side of the wine-red Gironde, each sloping bank echoing the sound. Lormont, so gracefully placed, holiday resort of rich Bordelais, sent on the signal; its neighbours higher up were not slow to follow. Swift, clear, sonorous, the alarum reached La Rochelle, fair as Cervantes' Dorothea seated by the brook, heroic as the warrior maid of Lorraine —thence it was borne along the salt marshes and thickets of Vendée—there more than anywhere needed the warning, 'The Patrie in danger.' Along the broad mouth of the Loire resounded the summons, by riverside village and village, in high tides of the 'Torrent révolutionaire,' islanded from the mainland; it passed, reinforced, given out with double, treble vehemence by Nantes—Nantes crowned with the glory of her Edict, but least beautiful, perhaps, of French capitals, despite superb situation and noble quays bordered with mansions of slaveowners, till yesterday traffickers in human flesh.

Through sombre, silent Brittany, and luxuriant, dance-loving Touraine, the Tocsin rang; it pealed forth from the glorious Creizker Tower of St. Pol de Léon, sweet little city, but sad, clothed in mourning livery of black and grey, reaching the island folk far off, summoning the men from their nets, the awestruck women to wayside Calvaries.

By road and river rang out the carillon, each modest belfry lending a voice, not a hamlet dumb. The fairy-like towns, with revolting memories, bordering Loir and Cher—Amboise, the beauteous, the bloodstained ; Blois, with its palace worthy of the Cæsars, like theirs also commemorative of lust and crime. By the vast cornlands of Beauce crept the sound. From the mountain-like mass of its cathedral, Bourges thundered forth—it was as if each glorious portico discharged notes of dread and warning. Across the heath-covered wastes and close-shut valleys of Marche pealed the solemn bell, following the sky-blue Indre as it meandered, full to the brim, through low-lying meads. The cloth-weavers of Chateauroux heard, and, quitting loom and fulling milk, flocked to the recruiting booth. By limestone cliffs and wooded hills, many a château rising above the green, by the chestnut woods environing the gloomy tower of Limoges, the Tocsin sped.

Rousing Auvergne, as if her volcanoes

suddenly opened, vomiting flame and fire, the sound reached the cutlers of Thiers in their sunless dwellings by the Durolle, euphemistic name of Stygian stream. Men livid with toil in perpetual twilight, begrimed with iron dust, not waiting to cast off leather apron and pull down shirt-sleeves, quitted their workshops, the younger and more ardent to return no more. There also a new voice made itself heard, the voice of mother country.

By swift, impetuous leaps, the sound rushed on towards Forez. As the mountain torrent here spanning chasm and gully, forcing tumultuous passage through lofty precipices, tossing aside pine-stem and boulder, so the Tocsin overcame every obstacle. Now it seemed to die away amid wide, unpeopled solitudes, then, on a sudden, clear, shrill, sonorous, from some valley hidden in mountain fastnesses, the watch-bell rang out afresh, startling the herds as they grazed, summoning their owners from the field. Zigzagging like lightning, meteor-like in its swiftness, intermittent, yet never lost, east, west, north, south, the cry of France went forth. From majestic Rhône, the river that brought Greece and Rome to Gaul, from the pearl-strewn shores of the Atlantic, whence rises Cordouan, the oldest lighthouse in Europe, from the storm-beaten cliffs facing England to the mule-tracks leading into Spain, from the barren promontories of Lozère to the rich vineyards of Champagne, the voice went forth, a voice new, yet clear, unmistakable, kindling every mind, thrilling every heart. She had spoken, France, the great mother, for her sons to hearken and obey!

All the village folks, Huguette's former neighbours, must of course go out to see the volunteers pass through. The march would take them by the prophetess's vineyard, that tiny possession, last to be put up for sale under the law of the Dead Hand. Mortmain and other feudal rights having now been abolished for ever, such lands became the property of the commune. Once again in the market, and this time legitimately, Félix and Douce had purchased it for Edmond and his bride. If only Huguette could have known that her fosterling, her darling, was here mistress after all! It was by such lessons as these that the peasant realised the Revolution.

Excitement and the crowd soon separated the four. As the Marseillaise, clouds of dust, and loud huzzas announced a detachment, Finette found herself alone, alone except for the white-capped, swaddled nursling in her arms.

Bareheaded despite the burning sun, with her neighbours, she leaned forward eagerly whilst the recruits marched by, not as yet in military order, here and there men falling back to bid kinsfolk or friends farewell.

The mother of a year was hardly less fair than the maiden. The look of patient sweetness still beamed from her blue eyes, the soft cheek showed dimples as before, but toils afield and matronly cares had already added years.

'Finette!' some one cried.

'Laurent, Monsieur Laurent!' was the astonished reply.

Finette and her old lover had never met since the solemn service under the Elms of Sully, although hearing news of each other from time to time. Laurent knew of her marriage with a peasant; Finette had learned that her sacrifice was not in vain, and that he would marry his rich bourgeoise.

The volunteers, unlike the former tatterdemalion soldiers of France, now wore uniform. Long blue riding-coat, top-boots, three-cornered hat, and tricolour sash added height and dignity to the former apprentice, as handsome and manly a fellow as any there.

'May you come safely home!' Finette got out amid rising tears.

The young man smiled coldly. Home to what? his face said.

'Are you happy, Finette?' he asked.

'My husband is good to me,' she replied, looking down, 'and I have this,' touching her child as she spoke. She glanced round, and, seeing no one near, added in low, agitated whispers—

'Listen, Laurent. By my innocent babe, I speak the truth. I went away without a word—I hid myself for your sake. I wanted you to become a bourgeois, to marry Mademoiselle Pernelle.'

Did he believe her? She hardly knew. He gazed a moment, then his eyes filled with tears, and, stooping down, he kissed both mother and child. He was yearning for sympathy and tenderness, and the little thing's confession somehow made him feel less lonely.

'There is another thing I wanted you to know,' she added, as he turned to go. 'I have never changed my religion, Laurent, the religion you taught me. And no one interferes with us Huguenots now; you and I may pray to God in the same way.'

'Yes, yes,' he replied.

'I hope you will come back,' she murmured.

'I hope I shall do my duty,' was the answer.

Then drums beat, the Marseillaise filled the air, hats and handkerchiefs were waved, flowers thrown to the victors of to-morrow. Amid indescribable tumult and emotion, the detachment passed on.

In her little salon Pernelle sat alone, almost for the first time throughout her entire existence doing nothing. Business was brisker. The universal enrolment had set mercers as well as tailors to work. At the sign of the 'Coiffe à Merveille' were supplied a dozen knick-knacks wanted for the soldier's kit, neckerchiefs, laced shirt fronts for officers, sashes and cockades.

This brief interval of idleness was stolen

from over busy hours. Why was Pernelle thus lazy, she who usually did several things at once? She sat with a piece of paper in her hand, apparently leaf torn from some schoolboy's exercise-book, reading, re-reading, and reading again. Those trite sentences, English tyro's attempt at French composition, were carefully put right in unmistakable French characters, and below the master had written his name. Wherein lay the fascination of this torn leaf for Pernelle's eyes? What made the perusal so absorbing, so magnetic? For an hour and more—the first idle hour of her life— she had been thus lost in reverie.

Whilst musing thus, she heard her uncle's voice just outside. The National Assembly dissolved, Nesmond's patriotic mission over, with the rest of his colleagues, he had returned to home and calling. He did not of set purpose avoid his niece; her formal engagement to Laurent evidently gave him intense satisfaction; but he remained icy cold. From the date of that interview with Velours, although outwardly on friendly terms, uncle and niece were strangers to each other.

Once or twice Pernelle had tried to break

through his reserve, win friendly hearing. He refused even to notice her overtures.

To-day his voice roused her as from a dream. She jumped up and opened the door.

'Berthe,' she cried, 'I *must* see your uncle. Bring him to me.'

The armourer, thrown off his guard, expecting some mere business discussion, entered with less frigid greeting than usual, even smiled as he sat down. But how unlike the smile of former years! Formerly he had glowed at the mere sight of his favourite, now she seemed in his eyes as any other.

Berthe dismissed, the door closed, Pernelle rose from her seat, clinging to him as a suppliant.

'Uncle!' she cried passionately, 'will you not relent? Think how lonely I am!'

'What woman's weakness is this, my niece? Your betrothed but takes his chance with the rest. The odds are that he may return General of Division.'

She quitted his side and sat down, still holding her torn leaf. One thing was clear— ever master of himself, sovereign of his will, he had set his face against reconciliation. He would stand by her and her sisters, in so far as worldly circumstances were concerned. They should never seek his advice, his protection, in vain. But toward Pernelle, once dear as his own child, he was relentless.

Purposely avoiding any allusion to Laurent, —the very mention of his name in her present mood seemed an insult to himself,—she got out—

'Uncle, there is no longer anything to keep us apart. You have not perhaps heard? He is in England—Louis de Velours. What harm can he do us there?'

'And what good?' was the scathing rejoinder. 'Has our country no enemies on foreign soil?'

'In him, no. Read this!' she cried; then, checking herself with sudden impulse, drew back, holding her sheet of exercise-paper still tighter to her heart. It was evidently sacred in her eyes. Keeping back indignant tears, she added, 'It was out of consideration for you, for me, that he threw aside his sword, put on civilian's garb, and crossed the sea. This scrap of paper tells everything. The marquis is earning his bread as a teacher of French.'

'And what is that to us?' said the armourer, rising. Anything like sentiment or weakness repelled him. He wanted the interview over, but before it was over she must clearly understand one thing. 'Is this a time to think of ourselves at all? Instead, every man, woman, and child of France must brace themselves to their daily tasks, the fulfilment of duty. Only thus can our poor country be saved. Saved it will, it shall be. I may not live to see the glorious day, the realisation of our hopes, nor, perhaps, may you either. The great day of freedom, brotherhood, prosperity, is sure to come. For each of us to hasten its advent.'

He stooped down, dropped a formal kiss on her forehead, and went away. Duty, duty! Pernelle repeated the words without as yet finding an echo in her heart.

She dared not weep. At any moment some intruder might surprise her. The luxury of a few idle minutes more she could not deny herself.

And once again that sheet of schoolboy's

copy-book, received a few hours before, was unfolded, devoured, covered with kisses. The sentences, evidently given as exercises, and carefully corrected, ran as follows :—

'To live ignobly, or what is called ignobly, may often be more heroic than to die magnanimously.

'Self-sacrifice, which includes the sacrifice of others, is but another name for egotism.

'Our great, our divine benefactors are those we love, whether or no they love us in return.

'Life is but another name for Hope. The word Adieu is meaningless on this side of the tomb.

'Corrected by Louis de Velours, French master at the school of Charterhouse, London, August, 179—.'

No word accompanied the leaf, which had reached Pernelle in a roundabout way. Evidently fearing to compromise her, Velours' missive came as envelope from a Cheapside mercer, the excuse being inquiry about certain Dijonnais specialities. Pernelle locked away the love-token and moved to the window.

From the narrow side street she saw the noble

façade of Nôtre Dame, and, high above, the Fleming keeper of time. As he raised his arm to signal noon, the sun emerged from a heavy cloud, the brilliant, bustling street was irradiated. All the townsfolk seemed abroad, young and old having flocked to greet the volunteers. One topic, and one only, was on every tongue—the threatened invasion of France and the newly-recruited armies moving towards the frontier. Yes, mused Pernelle, her uncle was right. No time now to dwell on self and selfish regret—or hopes! Duty must prove alike spur and staff, stimulant and healing; duty alone could save herself and every other sorrow-stricken creature, save France in her hour of peril.

Then she thought of her lover's words, 'Life is but another name for Hope. The word Adieu is meaningless on this side of the tomb.'

A commotion outside roused her. Streaming towards the Place d'Armes, again passed a procession, drums beating, flags flying, trumpets clanging, but all on a different scale. Only one queer martial figure was here visible, at his heels a band of ragged itinerant musicians, and all the little boys and girls of Dijon. The

hero of the hour was of course Fortuné, now recruiting on his own account, serving the purpose of ambulatory advertisement, looking up stragglers, enticing the recalcitrant. A proud man was the ex-smuggler, as he paraded the town, waving his hat to the citizens, shouting the watchword but a few days old, soon to be rendered so glorious—
'Vive la République!'

THE END.

www.ingramcontent.com/pod-product-compliance
Lightning Source LLC
Chambersburg PA
CBHW032009220426
43664CB00006B/184